Bravo Baryshnikov!

Bravo Baryshnikov!

Alan LeMond

With photographs by Lois Greenfield and others

Grosset & Dunlap
A Filmways Company
Publishers   New York

The publisher gratefully acknowledges permission to use the following:

"The Key." From *Modern Russian Poetry,* edited by Vladimir Markov and Merrill Sparks. Copyright © 1966, 1967 by MacGibbon & Kee, Ltd. Reprinted by permission of the Bobbs-Merrill Company, Inc.

Designed by Marcia Gloster Ben-Eli

First printing 1978
Printed in the United States of America

Contents

Le Grand Jeté West

In the crisp early-morning hours of June 30, 1974, just outside the stage doors of Toronto's O'Keefe Centre, perhaps the most brilliant classical dancer the Soviet Union has ever produced executed the great leap to the West. Mikhail Baryshnikov defected.

It was one of his greatest performances. Certainly it was his most successful. Choreographed brilliantly, executed flawlessly, typically daring — Mikhail Baryshnikov's Canadian premiere of "Le Grand Jeté West" stunned the ballet world.

His astounding solo, performed only once, contained elements of suspense and danger, and the ghostlike image of an impossible love story. It was in so many ways a tragedy. But in the main, it was a ballet of hope, of wonderful promise.

And it was real. For keeps. Baryshnikov could never go home again.

In ballet, a *jeté* is a leap in which the dancer pushes off the floor with one leg, makes an arc in the air, and lands on the other leg.

Theme and Variations was performed by Baryshnikov in 1974. The intricate Balanchine ballet was "the most difficult" he had performed since his great leap West.

In a *grand jeté,* the dancer leaps to the highest possible elevation. His leading foot is thrust up and out, and the leg with which he pushed off the floor reaches back and up to a high extension. A near-split is sometimes achieved in a *grand jeté.*

In Baryshnikov's *grand jeté* to the West, a complete split was achieved.

The Soviet ballet star had been a guest artist with a touring troupe of Moscow's Bolshoi Ballet. On the night of his defection, he and the other members of the Bolshoi had performed in Toronto and afterward had attended a reception in their honor.

The reception lasted until the wee hours of the morning, late for dancers, who must take good care of their bodies. Ballerinas and their male partners silently and wearily made their way toward the chartered bus that would return them to their hotel.

Suddenly, Baryshnikov turned away from the others and dashed toward a darkened car waiting two blocks away. In his anxiety to reach it he was nearly run over, but the powerful legs that had carried him to such great heights on stage served him well as he fled to freedom.

Baryshnikov had abandoned the Bolshoi tour. Henceforth, his career would go forward in the West.

Witnesses to his flight say that he was pursued by members of the KGB, the Soviet secret police. If so, they never caught him. Baryshnikov leaped into the getaway car and sped away into the dark Canadian night.

Eight days later, Baryshnikov issued a statement for the benefit of the press. "When I was in Toronto," he said from a secret refuge in Mississauga, just west of Toronto, "I finally decided that if I let the opportunity of expanding my art in the West slip by, it would haunt me always."

With him in his hideout was Christina Berlin. Christina is the pretty, young daughter of Richard Berlin, who for thirty-two years was president and chief executive of the giant Hearst publishing empire.

Christina's mother called the relationship between her daughter and the Russian dancer one of friendship. "They are very good, old friends."

Mrs. Berlin had met Baryshnikov in London and dined with him and Christina. She liked and admired him.

Baryshnikov confirmed Mrs. Berlin's evaluation of his and Christina's relationship. Christina was a good, close friend, someone he could call upon to help him out in a tight spot. When things got difficult for him, he asked Christina to stand by him.

Christina was in London when Baryshnikov telephoned his appeal for help. She responded immediately. In fact, so great was her rush that she arrived at London's Heathrow Airport without cash or credit cards and had to plead with strangers to cash her personal check so she could fly to Toronto.

Relaxed after dancing in a rehearsal with Canada's National Ballet shortly after his defection, the Soviet star signed to do two guest performances with the Toronto company.

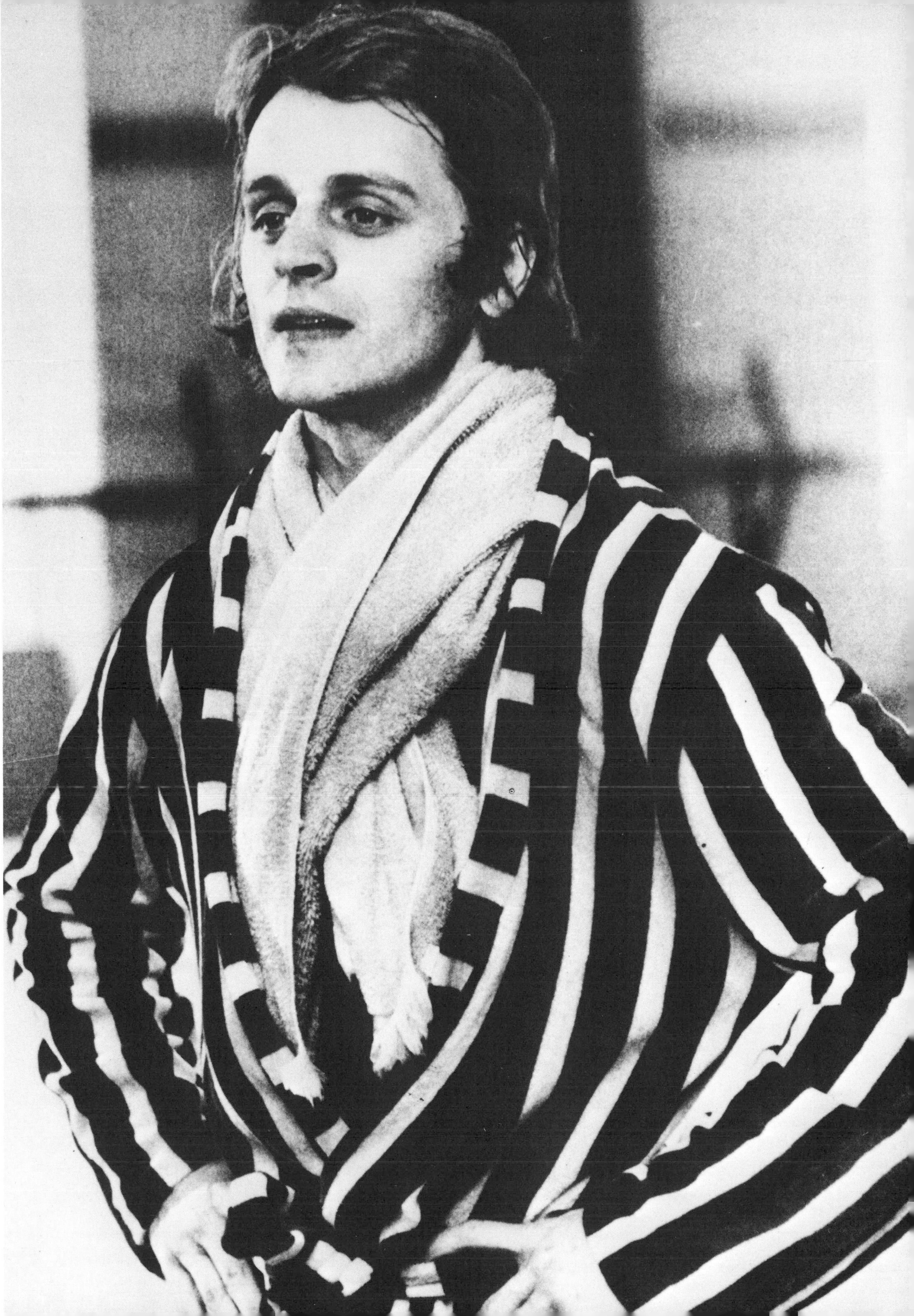

UPI Photo

UPI Photo

Romantic ties between Christina Berlin, the American girl who comforted him after he sought asylum, and the Soviet dancer were hotly denied by Baryshnikov. They were just "good friends."

Somehow she made it.

And they were together.

But not as a romantic team.

Baryshnikov was sincere in his praise of Christina. Few people have such friends in the world. But he was equally earnest when he begged reporters not to turn the friendship into a "bedroom drama."

Nevertheless, rumors and speculations about the pair abounded. Everyone, especially the press, loves a love story.

And so, from his first steps into the West, the specter of public curiosity has dogged Baryshnikov's heels and has invaded his private life. But he is a star. In the twentieth century, stars are not allowed to have private lives.

Christina was the first in what was to be a long list of sparkling women with whom he was romantically linked.

For her part, Christina followed the party line. She adamantly denied any love affair with Baryshnikov and implored people to be concerned with his talent, not his love life.

Still, most people wanted to know more about them as a couple. They had met four years before Baryshnikov's defection when they were introduced by ballet superstar Margot Fonteyn in London during a 1970 Russian ballet tour. They hit it off right away.

Some of the people who knew them felt that the two were more than just close friends — at least as far as Christina was concerned. One of her chums described Christina as "mad about him."

Why not? Baryshnikov is a small blond Russian with soulful eyes, incredible talent, and a magnificent body.

In 1971 Christina visited him in Leningrad where he was dancing with the Kirov Ballet. But he could not leave the city and she was convinced she would never see him again. After her departure, she wrote letters to him, but they were returned, unopened.

Despairing of ever persuading Baryshnikov to leave Russia, Christina returned to New York, giving up her job as Dame Margot Fonteyn's personal assistant.

She continued to follow the movements of the Russian ballet, and pictures of the Soviet ballet star adorned the walls of her Manhattan apartment. Shunning the social set to which she belonged, Christina dated a Russian correspondent and learned to speak some Russian.

A graduate of Manhattan's exclusive Chapin School, where aspiring stars learn to perform in the dramatic arts, Christina was also an occasional student at the Actor's Studio, the famed New York acting school that nurtured the talents of such stars as Marlon Brando and Shelley Winters.

Although dedicated to learning her craft, Christina was shy and quiet, avoiding her classmates. She was also a "Russian literature freak."

In 1972 Christina returned to London. She landed a job on the London edition of *Cosmopolitan* magazine. She stayed in close touch with the ballet world through her friends and connections in the Royal Ballet.

It was not unusual for her to do so, for she had always loved the ballet. And when Baryshnikov's call for help came, Christina was ready to answer it.

Christina was not involved in the actual escape plans. Baryshnikov asked her only to be with him during a difficult time. Perhaps he needed someone familiar to talk to in a new and unfamiliar world. He needed someone to be with him during the times when his exaltation turned to sorrow. He would leap about the room, excited to be free. Then, suddenly and unexpectedly, he would burst into tears.

It was difficult not to be at home. But he realized he had to make a choice between his art and his personal happiness.

The spells of weeping continued for a time after his defection. Friends say he was also uneasy in crowds. He feared being plucked away by the Soviet secret police.

Christina was a friend, a close friend, but the closeness between the American girl who loved the ballet and the Russian boy who was to become so famous in American ballet did not blossom into a romance. Over and over again, Baryshnikov repeated for the benefit of a doubting press that Christina was a friend, only a friend.

"There is absolutely no romance."

Despite this, stories persisted about a Baryshnikov-Berlin romance until, eventually, Christina faded out of the picture. Columnists commenting on the New York social scene now wrote that the Russian dancer was escorting one dazzling girl after another. By all accounts, he had adapted to a modern American life style.

Was he happy?

Yes, most times. But the life of a defector is not always the most pleasant situation.

He had to spend too much time defending himself, his motives, and his friends from rumors and speculations. Was Natalia Makarova involved in his escape? Did she not aid in the plans for his defection? No, she was not involved.

No, it was not political.

Not political?

No!

Baryshnikov stressed that his defection was not a political act. He was not a political person, and did not wish to become one.

Was it, then, for love?

Yes.

But not for the kind of love from which young girl's dreams are made, nor the kind on which romantic ballets are constructed, all gauze and illusion. It was for a more solid and lasting kind of love, more passionate, more consuming, more demanding. It was for the love of dance.

Baryshnikov had turned to a new world, had left Russia, for his artistic growth. As an artist, it was the only decision he could make.

He explained how, in Russia, a dancer's growth is stunted. New roles are rare. Everything happens slowly in Russia and, although some artists wait, others feel they cannot wait.

At first he hoped to be able to make guest appearances, perhaps to dance in ballets by Balanchine, Tudor, Robbins, and MacMillan. Had that been allowed, he would never have left Russia.

Russian dance tradition cuts two ways. Although classical ballet is preserved best in the Soviet Union, they stick closely to the rules. They observe them rigidly.

Several conditions in the world of Soviet dance in the early 1970s contributed to Baryshnikov's leap for "artistic freedom." Among them was a "ballerina crisis" in Leningrad; this occasioned a shortage of suitable partners at the Kirov for Baryshnikov. Choreographers of first-class talent also were in short supply, and the Soviet government refused to invite Western choreographers on the grounds that it was unpatriotic.

Nor did a dancer have the freedom to choose his own repertory. And little opportunity arose for him to dance in new ballets, especially ballets created for him.

Eager and exceptionally talented, the young artist Baryshnikov yearned to work with some of the West's choreographers.

He would have stayed in Russia if that possibility had existed — had he been able to go abroad and then return to dance with the Kirov. . . . If that situation had existed, he feels that no artist would have defected from Russia.

His strong yearning to try new ballets and new choreographers, to break free of the rigid classical mold, pushed him relentlessly toward the Western door. Finally, he went through.

Defection brings "a tremendous upheaval," in the words of Remi Saunder, an interpreter who befriended Baryshnikov and became a good friend. Remi likened Baryshnikov's Russian life to that of a bird in a cage. Open the cage, and the bird will fly out. No matter how poorly it is able to fly. Remi felt that Baryshnikov had no "survival muscles." Like a bird that has lived in a cage, he had to develop them or perish.

The West welcomed Baryshnikov with open arms. He was an instant celebrity. The idea that he would be denied asylum was not even considered. What was once the Star of the East became the Star of the West. Ballet heaven was rearranged.

On July 3, 1974, the newly defected Baryshnikov received permission to remain in Canada for at least six months on a special permit. The permit, good for a year, could be renewed after the first six-month period.

He would not need the extension. Before the end of July, Baryshnikov entered the United States under an "H-1" visa. This covers nonresidents of distinguished ability.

Baryshnikov lamented the bitter price he had to pay for his change of address. In Russia he was considered a criminal. Yet he realized that not to develop his great talent would have been an even greater crime.

Before Baryshnikov left Canada, the Canadian Department of External Affairs contacted him. The Soviet Embassy in Ottawa had requested their assistance in arranging a meeting between the twenty-six-year-old artist and a Soviet representative.

A few months later, an interesting rumor was confirmed. It dealt with the unique status of the defector.

To Mother Russia, Baryshnikov was not a criminal, not a defector. He could come home. All would be forgiven, all privileges would be restored. Apparently, a great dancer is above the petty rules of the great powers.

Baryshnikov heartily agreed with the opinion of the Soviets when they declared him "not a defector." He was, rather a "selector." He had selected art over personal well-being.

No doubt, the Kirov Ballet in Leningrad would sorely miss him. He was the leading dancer in a very strong ballet company. And, with the Bolshoi's Vladimir Vasiliev, Baryshnikov was one of the two top male dancers in Russia.

All things considered — he was *the* top.

Because there was a major difference between the two dancers. Vasiliev, thirty-four, was sliding down from his peak of power. Baryshnikov, only twenty-six, was entering upon the best years of his career.

The life of a dancer is not a long one.

Baryshnikov was not the first Soviet dancer to defect. Nor was he the first defector from the Kirov Ballet. It had lost Rudolf Nureyev in 1961, and Natalia Makarova in 1970. And Valery Panov and his wife, Galina Razina, after a long, internationally publicized struggle, were allowed to emigrate to Israel just two months before Baryshnikov defected.

Despite his intention to be free of any lasting entanglements with one ballet company, Baryshnikov — through the offices of Natalia Makarova — joined the American Ballet Theatre (ABT) in New York.

Daryl Dodson, ABT's manager, proudly announced the acquisition of the Soviet dancer. He would be a guest dancer for his first season; after that, they would discuss the future.

Over the next four years — before his second defection, of sorts — Baryshnikov danced *almost* exclusively for the ABT. He also danced spectacularly.

The *New York Times* dance critic Clive Barnes called his dancing "perfect," noting the special attention he paid to style, while keeping his dancing totally free of mannerisms. Barnes raved about the athletic strength and prowess of Baryshnikov's dancing — his astounding leaps. He added that only other dancers might truly see how closely Baryshnikov approached the supposed impossible.

Russia's loss was America's gain, and dance critics in 1974 said the 26-year-old Baryshnikov might someday outrank the highly esteemed Rudolf Nureyev.

The American Ballet Theatre was an excellent choice for Baryshnikov to have made. It had repertory roles he already knew and was also able to offer him new roles.

He danced what he knew and learned what was new to him.

As the ABT began the celebration of their thirty-fifth year, they were on top of the ballet world. They had the brilliant Baryshnikov with his unusual ability to fly through the air. And they had their own incredibly talented troupe of dancers.

They also had Gelsey Kirkland, who was a wondrous talent in her own right. Gelsey had joined the company at Baryshnikov's bidding. Talent attracts talent, and there was no doubt that he was talent.

He was flash.

He was dash.

UPI Photo

He was box-office.

Only a little over a month after his arrival, all of his performances were sold out, some even before the flyers were printed. The $15, $25, and $35 seats were gone first. Still available — for a short while — were the $50, $100, and $250 seats, the ones the general public could seldom afford.

When Baryshnikov made his first appearance in Washington, D.C., in July of 1974, he was partnered with Gelsey. Theirs was a magical partnership, one that would make them celebrated throughout the dance world.

Natalia Makarova once said that a good dance partner was one who could make her fall in love with him. She meant, of course, during the time when he was dancing with her.

Four Russian expatriates share a light moment in December 1974. Galina and Valery Panov emigrated to Israel after a two-year struggle. Nureyev and Baryshnikov sought creative freedom in the U.S.

Gelsey Kirkland joined the elite corps of Balanchine's
New York City Ballet and learned the challenging steps
of *Theme and Variations* from the master himself. Once
dancing the intricate movements of the ballet she
developed tendonitis. The intense pain caused her to
consider the impossible—giving up dancing.

Gelsey Kirkland joined the American Ballet Theatre at Baryshnikov's bidding. And together—on stage and off—they were magic.

Maybe Gelsey felt that way, too. But her feelings were projected beyond the footlights. Baryshnikov and Kirkland became partners in more than the dance.

Whatever their offstage relationship, on stage they were beautiful. They were — to put it blandly — tremendous.

Their Washington debut was a roaring success. Audiences shouted themselves hoarse, demanding repeated curtain calls. Bouquets of flowers littered the stage of the Kennedy Opera House as the enthusiastic ballet patrons showed their appreciation.

Kirkland was twenty-one. A former principal at the New York City Ballet, the bailiwick of Balanchine, she left City Ballet to dance with the ex-Kirov star because he asked her to.

It was a decision she might later have reason to regret.

Considered America's all-around best dance company, the ABT absorbed the spectacular talents of Baryshnikov without losing its balance — a good indication of its strength.

All was not smooth sailing, however. The artist from the USSR who dived into the receptive waters of the ABT caused a few ripples in the lake of ballet harmony. Some American dancers resented the little Russian for grabbing the spotlight so completely.

Dancer Ted Kivitt said candidly that Baryshnikov's timing hurt him. At thirty-two, Kivitt looked forward to the recognition for which he had worked hard. Instead, he saw his career taking giant steps backward. No longer would he be the star.

ABT ballerina Cynthia Gregory concurred. She felt that, as an American, she could offer nothing but her dancing. Yet, no matter how well she danced, she would not be awarded the recognition given to the Russian stars.

It is doubtful that anyone at the ABT resented the talent that Baryshnikov brought with him, however. Besides, he brought with him his Kirov schooling, classical perfection, and a stunning display of technical virtuosity. All of which he was willing to share.

Baryshnikov was open. Open to new ideas, new friendships. He wasn't afraid of taking risks or failing in new roles. And he took special pains to be just another member of the gang.

He was energy.

He was art.

But he was nevertheless resented.

No matter that it wasn't his fault if fame followed him around like his pet poodle. He didn't encourage that sort of attention (except from his dog). But it is hard to say that fame is wrong.

Talent should be recognized. How much better off would many of the world's now-famous artists have been if fame had accompanied their respective talents?

Consider everyone's favorite example, the artist Van Gogh.

In any case, press attention is not easily discouraged once it has spotted a personality worthy of the fuss. This is especially true in the center of the media, New York City. In the dance capital of the world, the media would pursue Baryshnikov.

But on the plus side for the ballet star, the media were also available to him, for his enjoyment and education. He eagerly investigated American plays, operas, and films. He especially appreciated television, watching all the old movies. He became a student of TV.

The pressure of life in New York bothered Baryshnikov, the furious speed with which New Yorkers burn up their time. He described the tempo in the Big Apple as ten times faster than it had been in Leningrad. He once commented that he liked Paris because "people have more time there than in New York."

Then, too, there was the language barrier. Although he spoke other languages besides Russian, in English Baryshnikov was not fluent.

Even so, it was "love at first sight." And in New York, coping with his new life and the pangs of separation from his home, Baryshnikov "became a man."

Surrogate parents helped him over the first hurdles: Remi Saunder and Howard Gilman, board chairman of the Gilman Paper Company.

Gilman, a patron of music and dance, lent Baryshnikov a Manhattan penthouse apartment rent-free. He and Remi Saunder introduced Baryshnikov to such artists as Mstislav Rostropovich and conductor Leonard Bernstein.

Rostropovich, also Russian, acclaimed as the greatest cellist in the world, was living in temporary exile. Baryshnikov and he had a common ground on which to meet and talk. They could discuss their homeland, which Baryshnikov sorely missed.

He would emphasize that he liked New York. Yet he could not call it home. To him, Leningrad always would be home.

It was hard — most painful — for Baryshnikov not to be able to return to Russia. Especially in the last few years at the Kirov, the management had been very good to him.

He had loved the Kirov and it had given him much. At times he wondered if he had made a mistake. Then he would see that he must take advantage of his opportunity in America.

"Anyway, what's done is done. There is no going back."

Prima ballerina Natalia Makarova, a defector in 1970, helped young Mikhail adjust to the American ballet world.

Entrée
Russian Roots

The *entrée,* or opening passages, in the life of the future ballet idol Mikhail Baryshnikov, began quietly in Riga, Latvia, on January 27, 1948. Like Balanchine's ballet *Theme and Variations,* his life had an understated beginning, full of serenity and peaceful grandeur. It also had moments of latent tension and restless energy — building up and up and up toward the inevitable climax.

Mikhail's parents were Russian. His father was an engineer, his mother a dressmaker. Tow-headed Mikhail's first childhood memory is of a sunny day in Riga.

He and his mother were outside. Unable to walk well as yet, he held on to her skirt for support. He remembers the dress she was wearing — a chiffon dress with yellow and purple flowers. To the young Mikhail, his mother, an ash-blond with bright blue eyes, was incredibly beautiful in the sunlight.

Baryshnikov's homeland is noted less for sunlight than for snow and vodka. But it is sunlight he remembers.

In 1969—five years before his defection—the Soviet star acknowledged the applause at the First International Competition for ballet dancers in Moscow.

Located in northern Eurasia and stretching from the Baltic to the Pacific, Russia lies three-fourths in Asia, the remainder in Europe.

To the west are Romania, Hungary, Czechoslovakia, Poland, Finland, and Norway. To the north is the Arctic Ocean. To the east is the great Pacific. To the south lie Korea, China, Mongolia, Afghanistan, Iran, and Turkey.

In area, Russia is the world's largest country, covering one-sixth of all land surface.

Latvia, where Baryshnikov was born, is one of the group of socialist republics within the Soviet Union. Technically the inhabitants of Latvia are Latvians, not Russians; but Baryshnikov's parents were Russian citizens, so Mikhail was Russian.

Latvia, with a population of approximately two and one-half million, is about the size of West Virginia, and has about the same population. Latvia was handed over to Stalin by Hitler as part of the German-Soviet Nonaggression pact that preceded World War II. The country was again taken over by Germany in 1941 and retaken by Russia in 1945. The Soviets retained Latvia after the war.

Despite all claims to the contrary, there is a class system in Russia. An upper class, a middle class, a lower blue-collar class, and a farming class are ascertainable. Although the Soviet class system is not based on inherited wealth or the private ownership of property, as is true in the United States, the Soviet classes are based on essentially the same things as those in America — status and power.

The upper class is composed of government bureaucrats (about six hundred thousand of them) who run the government and society. In the middle class are the specialists and professionals including writers, artists, high-level university professors, and scientists. The lower classes — as is often the case — are made up of farmers and manual laborers.

Baryshnikov was firmly in the middle class.

Both powerful nations, Russia and the United States share certain qualities. Courage, energy, and humor can be found in the citizens of both countries. But the countries are different. Russians and Americans have different mentalities and take different psychological approaches to life and living.

Decisions are reached differently, too. And, of course, the politics of the two countries are definitely in opposition. Thus Americans and Russians often find it hard to understand each other.

Yet, when he was growing up, Mikhail thought little of all that. He skipped along the shores of the ancient Baltic Sea and had a very happy childhood. He ran, leaped, swam, and kicked a football. He was an active child. He hated to sit still.

Besides football, he tried fencing and gymnastics. He even sang in the children's choir.

He tried piano lessons, too. He modestly says he was "very bad."

Bad or not, his childhood dream was to be a concert pianist and play with a large orchestra. His mother changed that dream — and ballet history — when she took her energetic young son to the Latvian Opera School to take the entrance exam.

Baryshnikov recalls that he liked it right away. Theater interested him from the start.

Mikhail was twelve at the time, a relatively late age for a dancer to begin his study. Most serious students start at age seven or eight.

He admits he did not take dancing seriously at first. His was more the interest of a dilettante. Soon, however, he began to glimpse the challenge dancing held for him.

He had tried many sports and at one time wanted to be a gymnast. But he hated discipline. And although good at school academically, he found it hard to sit still in school.

With this temperament, dancing was difficult for him to study seriously. But he liked the challenge.

The ballet was not particularly understandable for the twelve-year-old Mikhail, but the mystery dared him. Dared him to understand with both his mind and his body.

By the end of his first year of training, all his other activities became secondary. They would soon disappear altogether. Dancing would replace all else. After his first performance, he couldn't tear himself away from the ballet.

Most exciting was the reaction of the audience.

Gradually, the difficulty of learning eased.

He wanted to learn and had very good teachers. He saw it as a great chance — maybe his last. Before he was fourteen, he knew what he was working for. By sixteen, dancing was a necessary part of his life.

Tragedy entered his life when he was thirteen. His mother died.

His father remarried soon after.

Perhaps this trauma in his life made him turn to the ballet as a solace for his grief. Dancing was what his mother had led him to. And it was a comfort to him.

The raw energy dance consumed could take his mind away from the emptiness in his heart. He was forced to concentrate on the physical stress he was imposing on his body.

And he danced. And he danced.

The dance, something he liked, became something he loved.

Besides dancing, he studied French and other subjects — many of

UPI Photo

Stately buildings comprising the Admiralty line the banks of the Neva River, which flows through Leningrad. Cut by numerous canals and streams, the city has more than six hundred bridges.

them relating to the ballet. The Latvian Opera School had then — and still has — high scholastic ranking.

At fifteen, Mikhail was invited to join a troupe of dancers who toured and performed for teen-agers.

A stop on the tour brought the adolescent Mikhail to the old Czarist capital of Leningrad, formerly Saint Petersburg. The classic charm of the city was like heady wine or good Russian vodka.

He wanted to stay.

He strolled down Nevsky-Prospekt, one of the most famous avenues in the world. The Hermitage was there, full of treasures. The Winter Palace. The Cathedral of Saint Isaac.

He had to stay.

Perhaps this strong desire to live in Leningrad gave the young man the courage to do what he did next.

He applied for admission to the famed Kirov School of Ballet.

The Kirov had nurtured such greats as Nijinsky, Pavlova, Karsavina,

Danilova, Balanchine, and Nureyev, all of whom were giants in the history of world ballet.

Alexander Pushkin, who taught at the Kirov school, was one of the greatest of all Russian male ballet teachers. He had also been the teacher of Nureyev, who had defected three years before Mikhail applied to study at the Kirov. The two great dancers were not to meet until they were introduced in New York in 1974.

When he attended a dance class at the Kirov school, young Mikhail was overwhelmed by the desire to be a Kirov student. He approached Pushkin and said simply, "I would very much like to be your pupil."

The great Pushkin allowed the boy to dance for him.

"I was like a young goat knocking over tables and chairs," Baryshnikov recalls.

But Pushkin studied the boy carefully, then took him downstairs to the school's doctors. They checked him over thoroughly, the way they would a race horse. They probed and poked.

Pedestrian and auto traffic are heavy along famed Nevsky-Prospekt, a main shopping area in Russia's second largest city, the beloved home of Mikhail Baryshnikov.

Apparently they liked what they found, for Baryshnikov was admitted to the Kirov School of Ballet. Personable, full of good humor, and bursting with talent, the young man's potential was obvious.

Admittance was not to be immediate, however. He had to spend the summer in Riga awaiting final approval.

Baryshnikov says that it would have been "shattering" if he had not been accepted. He spent the summer mentally living the life of the Kirov. Leningrad and the school alike were electrifying for him. He could not imagine living apart from them.

He tried to relax by fishing — a sport he still enjoys — but it is doubtful that his heart was totally running with the fish that anxious summer.

He waited.

Then came word to gladden his soul. He was accepted.

Pushkin taught only a few boys at a time, and young Baryshnikov was to be one of them. He had been accepted into the Kirov school, into Pushkin's "class of perfection."

It was wonderful for Baryshnikov. He acquired an excellent start toward the mastery of classical dance, ballet history, acting, mime, and fencing in the three years he boarded at the Kirov.

He also acquired a nickname — Misha. The name was given to him by Pushkin, and today Baryshnikov is generally and affectionately known as Misha to his friends and fans.

Misha sometimes lived with Pushkin and his wife. He became almost a son to the teacher; in turn, Misha looked upon the Pushkins as his family, for his own mother was dead, and his father lived far away in Riga.

But, above all, Misha was a student, a student of the legendary Pushkin.

It was a great responsibility even to be Pushkin's student, for Pushkin was acknowledged as a great teacher. A Pushkin student who could not do a step had no one but himself to blame.

Misha, and the other students, worked from nine in the morning until ten at night. Sweating, straining, and stretching tight muscles. Misha continued his studies in French and to them added makeup, and Russian and Western literature.

The Kirov school is famous for its instruction in acting although, by Western standards, the acting is highly stylized. The Kirov instructors are especially noted for their skill in teaching mime.

At the age of eighteen, Baryshnikov was admitted to the full Kirov regimen. By that time he had spent three years in Pushkin's "class of perfection."

Misha was assigned to solo roles without having to fight his way up through the ranks of apprentices who serve in the corps de ballet, which

The good-humored, immensely likable ballet idol acquired the nickname Misha from his great teacher Pushkin at the Kirov Ballet school.

is the chorus of a ballet company.

This was a highly unusual move — one reserved only for the best. Nijinsky (considered one of the finest male dancers who ever lived), Pavlova, and Nureyev were predecessors of Baryshnikov who shared this high esteem.

A state-supported organization with a company of more than two hundred dancers, the Kirov had a repertory at the time of Baryshnikov's leaving of only twenty-six ballets — small by Western standards.

Because they had so few ballets and so many dancers, and because in Russia the theater must share space with the opera, Baryshnikov danced only three or four times a month.

Nevertheless, in 1967, when he was only nineteen, tales of the Russian whirlwind who commanded the stage and leaped to incredible heights began to be told in the West. On a trip to the Soviet Union that year, the dance critic Clive Barnes described the talented Misha as an *almost* flawless dancer.

Barnes felt the young dancer lacked the strength that would come with age. He also found Baryshnikov's dancing less exciting than some. But he recognized in Misha "a dancer of whom the world will hear more."

The five-foot, seven-inch boy wonder performed hypnotically. Barnes noted that more "attention was drawn to the strange, serious-looking boy than I had ever seen before." The fair hair, the frown of intense concentration, the "unaffected perfection" were all recorded.

In 1970 Baryshnikov danced for Western audiences for the first time — in London and again in the Netherlands. He was enthusiastically acclaimed. His performances away from home were a triumph.

But not completely.

His tastes, it was noted, ran to Western clothing and Western women. This was not something to be applauded by the political leadership in the USSR. It was something with which to be concerned.

Baryshnikov felt the baleful stare of disapproving Soviet eyes.

He was watched.

In 1970 there was also tragedy in store for him.

His teacher, Pushkin, died.

Baryshnikov was to be his last great pupil. And the young artist was to miss Pushkin sorely. Of his teacher he said he was "a pure and simple character."

Baryshnikov respected Pushkin immensely, comparing him to "somebody who stepped out of an icon." He indicated that it was Pushkin who turned his love of dance into a passion.

Describing Pushkin as "a father to me," Baryshnikov recalled his teacher as a man with "amazing gentleness and sensitivity, a desire to help his students." Above all, said Baryshnikov, "he was a person."

The classes that Pushkin taught had not been noticeably different from others' classes. But the great teacher had — through inherent ability and sheer work experience — become so steeped in his profession that he wore it like a second skin.

He steered rather than pushed his students, and he never forced a dancer to do what he didn't want to do. He brought out the best in each dancer, but he took no credit for it. His students' successes belonged to them, not to Pushkin.

Pushkin died in the streets of Leningrad in 1970. Saddened by the loss of his friend and teacher — his "almost father" — Baryshnikov transformed his sorrow into positive action. He offered to take over Pushkin's class.

He was permitted to do so.

Misha tried to pass on what he had been taught, "the most logical series of steps and movements" he had ever seen.

Would Baryshnikov have left Russia if Pushkin had not died?

Who knows? Only Baryshnikov. And he has not supplied the answer.

But it seems logical to assume that Pushkin's death made it easier for Misha to leave. There was no longer anything to hold him back. His mother was dead; he was not close to his father (geographically, at any rate); now, Pushkin was gone.

For seven years before his defection, Baryshnikov was the ballet idol of the Soviet Union. He was the youngest performer ever to receive the State Award of Merit. In 1966, when he was eighteen, he won the gold medal at the Varna international competition in Bulgaria. He repeated his triumph in 1969 in Moscow.

In 1969 a ballet solo was created for him. Choreographer Leonid Jacobson composed *Vestris*. In the solo, Baryshnikov portrayed the great eighteenth-century French dancer Auguste Vestris, who has been called the God of Dance.

A fitting role for Misha.

In his daily life Baryshnikov did not act the part of rebel. He made no trouble. He had little reason to do so, actually. He made a good salary and had a fine apartment, a maid, and other fringe benefits, including a car. He lived well.

Still, it wasn't enough.

Although he had everything the system could offer him, it wasn't easy for him.

Dances he wished to dance, music he wanted to set to choreography, did not conform to the official taste of the ideology committee. They were "not suitable for the ballet."

Theme and Variations, in Balanchine's neo-classical style, demands strict control and enormous power from the dancers. Baryshnikov found the strain on his legs "incredible."

There was also a certain lack of spice in his life. As Remi Saunder put it, "There you are given food, but not a choice of food."

Russian artists are treated very well materially, but they have little chance to experience the natural highs and lows that come with the use of one's own initiative.

Still, it must have come as a shock to the KGB when the ballet idol "who had everything" decided to scratch the itch in his feet and wander off to foreign lands, to see what lay far beyond the Urals.

He had everything. They must have asked themselves: what more could he want?

Not fame, certainly. He had that.

Not adoration, either. He had that, too. In Leningrad he was besieged by women who worshiped him.

And it wasn't for great honor. Weeks before he defected, a gala was held at the Kirov, and a whole evening of dance was dedicated to him.

He danced three new ballets.

But other things were not so nice. One of his favorite roles was *The Creation of the World,* which was based on drawings by Jean Effel. In it, Baryshnikov danced seminude.

"*Nyet!*" cried the cultural minister. "Is too sexy. Is too trivial."

It was back to the drawing board for *The Creation of the World.* The ballet must adhere to official taste. And the spectrum of artistic approval was extremely narrow.

The artist within Baryshnikov burned.

He had suffered silently and stoically over minor irritations. But to be censored artistically was a *divertissement.* A dance without plot. Without message. A dance of form only.

In vain he tried to say that ballet changes constantly, that generations change. Limitations, too, should change.

Art, Baryshnikov believes, should be above politics. The language of art is a common language. Audiences are the same everywhere in the world. When the dancing is good, audiences are enthusiastic, no matter what country you are in.

So Mikhail Baryshnikov, dancer *extraordinaire,* left his homeland, for art's sake, and proceeded to conquer the Western dance world.

He could see how Natalia Makarova and Rudolf Nureyev had grown as artists after they left Russia. He, too, wished to grow.

The finely honed precision of his classical Russian training is beautifully apparent in this shot of Misha performing in *Theme and Variations*.

The Reluctant Celebrity
Pas d'action

It is probably unfair, and certainly downright frivolous, but Mikhail "Misha" Baryshnikov is better known to the American public for his natural, unaffected predilection for beautiful women than for his fantastic technical skill in the performance of ballet.

Well, that's not exactly true.

Not any longer.

Now he is best known for his role of Yuri in *The Turning Point,* a role for which he won an Oscar nomination.

He was amazed. For acting?

Is joke, no?

If they had given him the nomination for dancing, well, that would be a different story. But for acting?

He thought of the role as good experience. But he is not a professional actor. He compared his being picked for the part with the old story of the director who makes a star out of someone with a photogenic face and a stronger-than-usual personality.

Judith Jamison of Alvin Ailey's City Center Dance Theater does the "Hustle" with Misha on a Manhattan penthouse terrace. They were announcing their upcoming dance alliance to photographers and reporters.

He was shocked when he saw his first rushes.

He felt he was terrible. But Herb Ross, the film's director, reassured him when he said all actors who look at rushes for the first time are horrified.

The film, of course, added greatly to Misha's celebrity status outside the close-knit world of ballet. Baryshnikov found himself a superstar.

Nora Kaye, the former ballerina who is married to Herb Ross, predicted that Baryshnikov would get other offers to act.

"I wonder if he will take them," she mused.

Yes, he is definitely a superstar. But does he like it?

He is living, he says, his own life. If people stop him on the streets or send him letters, what can he do?

Nevertheless, he confesses that at times it bothers him very much.

Which is probably an understatement.

Baryshnikov is a serious man — albeit the seriousness is laced with a strong shot of humor — and if he could have his way, he probably would prefer being left alone.

For sure, he had said often enough that he would not mind it one bit if the press let him be. If the hullabaloo were not so noisy or so undignified.

Robert Redford once courageously informed a roomful of reporters that he was not a public person. He felt that the fact that he was an actor did not mean that he must automatically share his private life with the public.

"I owe the public a performance," he said, and added that it's up to them to decide whether they like it or not. His private life he considered his own.

Well, perhaps.

Perhaps not.

Can you separate the artist from his art? The dancer from the dance?

In any case, Baryshnikov's activities, and speculations about his activities, appeared regularly in the press. Not only in gossip columns and scandal sheets, either. In the "respectable" press.

He is the "Travolta of High Culture," bannered *People* magazine.

His "blue-gray eyes have 'an over-ripe' look and hint at unreported night-time activity," said *New York* magazine.

A writer for the *New York Times* claimed Baryshnikov's eyes gave "mute testimony to too much work or unknown night-time pleasures."

He likes to play, reported *Time* magazine in its 1975 cover story. *Time* noted that, despite Baryshnikov's revelation that he is drawn to "sad ballets, sad feelings," he can be the life of a party.

Well, he plays the piano and is an excellent mimic. And once, at a party for the ABT in Texas, he and several other male dancers skinny-

dipped in the pool. When a young woman dancer entered the pool, he led the group that helped her take off her bathing suit.

He is basically one of the guys. He will wait his turn for a shower, buy champagne for a special occasion, and join in any celebration. He eases tension by humorous diversions, such as belting out a rousing rendition of show tunes, or just playing the fool. He uses his excellent ability as a mimic to make people laugh. He loves harmless practical jokes like blackening his teeth, as he did as Yuri in *The Turning Point.*

But, despite this openness, this desire to see people happy and relaxed, he is alone much of the time. He compares himself to a "wolf lost from the pack."

He is so busy that he has made very few good friends. He feels that it takes years to develop deep friendships.

He is no longer afraid that if he answers a knock at his door late at night, he will be whisked away by the secret police. He is no longer afraid in crowds. Still, he is most comfortable in the company of other Russian émigrés, in the intimate setting of small dinner parties.

Baryshnikov, the movie star, jokes with co-star Leslie Browne in a scene from *The Turning Point.* Both were nominated for Oscars for their debut performances.

At home he plays the stereo, recites Russian poetry — Pasternak, Mandelstam, Pushkin (no relation to his teacher) — and laughs at Florence Foster Jenkins's eccentric operatic high-jinks.

He does not cook. He claims that standing at a stove would be "terrible" for his legs.

He drinks vodka, Scotch and soda, or Heineken beer.

He is an occasional smoker, but he is trying to cut down.

Partial to French, Russian, and hot Chinese Szechwan dishes, he also likes American steak and salad.

Sweets are not for him.

Offstage he is sometimes moody. Brooding. His personality has been known to change abruptly. His sunny disposition is suddenly obscured by dark gray clouds of gloom. He becomes quiet, withdrawn.

He loves dogs. He was heartbroken when he had to leave his dog behind in the Soviet Union. He now has a large black poodle, which he calls La Goulue, after the notorious dancer who was one of Toulouse-Lautrec's favorite subjects.

Louise Weber was the real name of the blonde Alsatian laundress who reached fame and notoriety at the Moulin Rouge. One of Lautrec's most famous posters, that of the strawberry blonde in the brown and white polka-dotted blouse, kicking up her heels, is of La Goulue.

Baryshnikov has been overheard referring playfully to his poodle as a "dirty garbage rat" as he tickles her ears.

Misha is adorable, talented, and also one of the most highly paid dancers in the world. It's little wonder that many women desire him. He radiates sexiness, onstage and off.

Is that a nice feeling?

He admits that, for him, it is "important."

Perhaps it is at that.

But he does not care to be asked about how it feels to be a sex symbol. Questions dealing with that taboo subject go unanswered — usually. And a storm brews behind the cool blue eyes.

He makes no secret of the fact that he "adores women." When asked his opinion of American women, he describes them as "much tougher than usual."

And then he qualifies that statement. "Tougher" is the wrong word. He means "much stronger mentally."

Does he, then, like stronger women — mentally?

Ummmm.

He admits he likes the "image of energy" stamped on American women. That is, he likes it up to a "normal" level. He does not mean women in "leather jackets."

There are gaggles of women who don't wear leather jackets, and Baryshnikov's name is kept alive in the gossip columns by their attention to him. Or vice versa.

One pundit, terming Baryshnikov the year's hot young superstar, added that "he always gets the girl."

Baryshnikov complains that his private life has become some sort of symbol. "I'm not the first straight dancer, nor the last," he protests.

He certainly is not.

But he is the most vivid, the best known. He is — to most — the epitome of the masculine ballet dancer.

Edward Villella, a principal at the New York City Ballet, did a great deal toward breaking the stereotyped image of the effeminate male ballet dancer. And this was long before Baryshnikov entered the scene.

Villella came to the dance indirectly. His first love was sports. He was injured while playing in a sandlot baseball game. His sister's ballet classes would offer more supervision, his mother felt.

He studied until he was fifteen. Then he went to the New York State Maritime College, earning a Bachelor of Science degree in marine transportation, playing baseball, and becoming the campus welterweight boxing champion.

He returned to dancing as therapy after a barroom injury.

This time, he was serious about his dancing. He joined the City Ballet in 1957, when he was twenty, and became a principal.

And he proceeded through a great ballet career.

Villella at one time was a part owner of the discothèque Arthur, and he heartily enjoyed his bachelorhood after his seven-year marriage to Janet Greschler broke up. His ex-wife — who is also an ex-dancer — and he have one child, Roddy, age nine.

But it was Baryshnikov, not Villella, who reached far into the hinterlands of America and changed the ballet dancer's image for all time.

"You know what this fantastic little Russian is going to do? He's going to make it respectable for American boys to be dancers." So says a character in *The Turning Point*.

If that line was not written about Baryshnikov, it could have been.

When you ask him about the image assigned to him by the public, he indicates that the role does not please him.

It is a terrible cliché, he claims, that ballet dancers are thought of as being homosexual. It has no relevance, anyway.

Who cares? is the viewpoint of Baryshnikov. To him, dancers, like anyone else, should live their lives in the way they want. And be happy. That's it.

He states firmly that he is responsible only for himself.

He does not want to discuss "right" and "wrong." He is not a lawyer or clergyman.

But he certainly doesn't hide the fact that he likes women.

"This is not worst reputation," he adds.

No. But, for a ballet dancer, it is unusual.

Dancer Ted Kivitt agrees that it *shouldn't* matter what the sexual preference of a dancer is, but he knows that the stigma still exists.

Kivitt thinks things have changed somewhat, but a male in the ballet is still stigmatized. He recalls that when he asked his girl to marry him, her brother flew up from Texas to meet him. Says Kivitt, "He had his doubts."

After brother and brother-in-law-to-be met, the union between Ted Kivitt and Karena Brock, both principals at the ABT, was fully approved.

Obviously, and as is true for the rest of the population, there are different life styles for different dancers.

Baryshnikov's life style, for instance, is unrestricted by matrimonial ties.

He has conducted affairs with many women, often with dancers he has worked with. And some of these friendships have ended with chilly abruptness.

Misha, it has been said, rapidly worked his way through the corps de ballet at the American Ballet Theatre. Left strewn in his wake were brokenhearted would-be Giselles. Lately, Hollywood stars are said to be succumbing to his abundant charm.

Has the young Romeo from Riga really left a trail of broken hearts as he worked his way through the ranks?

A former ballerina girl friend of Misha's admitted that she, like others before her, knew the relationship wouldn't last, but added pensively, "Who could resist?"

Gelsey Kirkland apparently was one who couldn't.

The ballerina Misha once compared to a finely cut polished diamond — one of the most exciting ballerinas dancing today — joined him as his partner at the ABT.

Gelsey had met Misha in 1972 when she was touring with a City Ballet company through Russia. She saw him perform there. In the summer of 1974 she journeyed to Toronto to watch the Bolshoi, with which Misha was performing. At supper afterward, they renewed their brief acquaintance and grew to like each other.

Gelsey was an ideal size to be partnered with Baryshnikov. Her "almost five-foot-four" is a neat match for his "almost five-foot-seven."

And she was definitely talented enough to be his partner.

Perhaps the thought of a possible partnership entered Baryshnikov's mind at that time.

Gelsey and Mikhail dance the *pas de deux* (a dance for two) from *Don Quixote* with the Pennsylvania Ballet Company at the Brooklyn Academy of Music. Mikhail loves this "crazy Russian salad of a ballet."

UPI Photo

Above & right: As the lusty, high-spirited barber, Basil, Baryshnikov woos the innkeeper's daughter, Kitri. The romance between Kirkland and Baryshnikov sparkled on stage and off.

Perhaps it entered her mind also.

When Gelsey received a call from one of Baryshnikov's associates asking her to dance with him, now that he had elected not to return to the Soviet Union, she was instantly receptive.

Would she dance with him?

"Of course I will!"

And she did.

Onstage — together — they dazzled. Offstage — together — they were electric. The togetherness turned into a love affair.

Gelsey, perhaps as dedicated in the pursuit of perfection in their common art as Baryshnikov, held her own opinions about professionalism in dance. Some of her views differed from Baryshnikov's. High-voltage discussions ensued about individual approaches to technique and style.

Perhaps this professional tension contributed to the eventual breakup. In any case, Misha — like the character Yuri in *The Turning Point* — moved on to others.

The parting hurt her.

But Gelsey recovered.

She recovered not only from the break with Baryshnikov, but from other problems as well. She suffered through a weight problem (at one time she weighed less than 90 pounds), which caused her to lose the ballerina role in *The Turning Point* to Leslie Browne. She also went through a frustrating psychological conflict about her feelings for the ballet. She both loved the dance and resented it. The opposing emotions were pulling her apart. But rewarding sessions with physical therapists, physicians, and dance teachers helped her to pull her act together. Today Gelsey is better adjusted and more respected than she has ever been, winning praise from both Baryshnikov ("she advances from performance to performance") and Rudolf Nureyev ("she has that beautiful fluidity in her movements and an incredible strength for such a small girl").

She also moved on to a pleasant, comfortable relationship with tall, blond ABT soloist Richard Schafer.

There is no reason whatsoever to blame Baryshnikov for any of Gelsey's problems. Even as a little girl Gelsey was headstrong and determined to take on the world.

Her mother, joking about Gelsey's grit and drive, once said her daughter had come out of the womb marching.

Nor was Baryshnikov responsible for Gelsey's disappointment after the bright flame of their relationship flickered and went out.

He says with a sigh, "I make no promises."

Another of Baryshnikov's non-ballet occupations is reading. Aleksandr Solzhenitsyn is a writer whose books fill him with emotion — a sense of awe and *tristesse*, a sweet sadness.

And, of course, he likes Russian poetry.

Mandelstam, one of his favorite poets, wrote the following lines in his poem *Tristia:*

> I've learned the science of farewells — at night
> When those unloosened-hair laments are wept. . . .

Undoubtedly, Baryshnikov has enjoyed the sad feelings the poem evokes, and has perhaps pondered the significance of the final lines:

> We shall remember even in Lethe's cold
> That Earth cost us as much as ten heavens.

Perhaps he has also pondered and enjoyed the poem *The Key,* which was written by an anonymous Russian poet. It's a hearty Russian borscht of a poem. Full of life, but tinted with the beet-red melancholy of a heavy heart.

I was a bachelor — I lived by myself.
I had a room with a private door.
And whenever I got in a certain mood,
I invited a visitor.
My friends lived with their mothers-in-law
And with wives from the same grain . . .
Either too fat or too thin,
Monotonous and gray like rain.
And every year — having aged one year
Bearing kids of either sex,
The wives became statues in long bread lines
With nooses around their necks.
And all my friends loved their wives;
They used to ask me this:
Why don't you marry? You Playboy, You!
What do you know of married bliss?
My friends didn't like their wives;
They liked girls with soft, young hands
And with eyes into which like a stone one falls,
And falls and falls and never lands.
I was squeamish (you remember, no doubt)
I didn't ask stupid questions; I knew how to behave . . .
I simply gave them the key to my room;
That's what they asked for — and that's what I gave.

What do they see in him, this ballet Adonis? How do those ladies who adore him describe him?

"He's a dream," says one.

"He's wonderful," says another.

Yet, one's first impression can be disappointing. He seems chunky, his muscles are overdeveloped, and he has a somewhat rounded back. Nor does he have the magnetism of a Rudolf Nureyev.

He may lack the electric personality of Nureyev, but women do not seem to miss it.

"Stripped of stage make-up, he looks even younger and more vulnerable, with pale skin and those huge, dreamy eyes," cooed Joanna Ney in *Cosmopolitan*.

Women all see the same man, at least the essence of the same man. And in that essence, he is Prince Charming.

His short stature doesn't matter — not even to tall women — and certainly not to petite, lacelike ballerinas. Ballerinas such as Leslie Browne.

Leslie co-starred with Misha in *The Turning Point,* and rumors of a romance between the two flew about the movie set. Then she watched as Baryshnikov showed up with actress Jessica Lange at a party thrown to celebrate the end of filming.

Like a typical Aquarian (he was born under the sun sign Aquarius), Baryshnikov does not seem the type to settle down with one woman.

Aquarians don't take to marriage too readily, according to the astrologers. Most of them "avoid it as long as it's humanly possible," says Linda Goodman in her popular book on astrology, *Sun Signs.*

Aquarians are always seeking — one more experience, one more experiment. But they are also known to have high ideals. Perhaps this is why they desire change and are often controversial.

What does Aquarian Baryshnikov enjoy besides the ballet, poetry, and women? What would he do if he weren't a dancer? If it gets to the point where he can no longer dance?

He doesn't know. He thinks he might enjoy raising dogs. He likes fishing. He can see himself involved in the business end of ballet. . . .

At present, however, "dancing is a necessity for me."

He doesn't want to make any more movies. Not now.

An interesting director and an interesting subject might well change his mind. He cannot say he will never make another film. Who knows?

He has not, for all time, ruled out the possibility. But his enthusiasm for films is not at fever pitch.

Part of the reason for not wanting to make another movie may be his reaction to his first film. He cannot shake the feeling of strangeness he experienced.

Filming is very difficult for a dancer. There is too much waiting, too much stillness.

He found it interesting meeting professional and talented actresses such as Anne Bancroft and Shirley MacLaine. And watching them work.

But he found it difficult dancing in front of a camera.

He also found it hard to keep his dancer's body in shape. Some days the shooting went on from seven in the morning until midnight.

There was also the bureaucratic chain of command to contend with. Everything that went on in the filming involved unions, and in order to have a successful, cooperative crew, the threads between unions and producers had to be tightly interwoven. If one weak thread broke, the whole cloth unraveled.

Last, but certainly not least, there was the language problem.

Misha's mind must work with computerlike efficiency for him to speak his lines correctly, translating English to Russian to English. Unless he can grasp the point of phrases, it is just so much phonetics.

He must know the meaning! There he goes again, being a perfectionist. Deciding to do something, then doing his best.

But it all paid off, and he received high praise from director Herb Ross.

Ross thinks Baryshnikov has already made the transition from dancer to actor. He recognized how nervous the dancer was during the first read-through of the script. But Ross also saw "the intelligence and instincts of a superior artist." Baryshnikov realized that there was a huge difference between projecting a role on stage and behaving more naturally in front of a camera. He also knew how to improvise. And his ability to ad lib was a tremendous advantage.

Somehow, in spite of the many problems, the whole project blended together and the company brought forth a masterpiece, a multicolored tapestry.

Not flawless, but beautiful.

Even in the distinguished company of the cast of *The Turning Point,* the dancer who played Yuri stood out.

Herb Ross called it "wit and charm in the movie sense." This opinion was rousingly seconded by critics, audiences, and the Oscar-nominating committee.

But Baryshnikov does not care much about that praise. He cares only about his image as a dancer, and about what his friends think of him.

He knows he cannot care about the whole world.

Yet, despite the hounding of fame, all the futile attempts to open his heart for publication, he says he is happy — and lucky.

"I am the luckiest man."

Maybe he is.

The Artist
Danseur Noble

You do not observe Baryshnikov the first time you see him dance — you absorb him. He is unique. Dazzling. Unbelievable. Positively overwhelming.

He is a genius, and like all geniuses, he conjures up his magical reality from a bubbling blend of 99 percent perspiration and one percent inspiration. A potent combination.

There may be some luck involved, but hardly enough to be noticed. In the main, dancing is dedicated hard work.

Baryshnikov recognized this as a student. It was a hard job, he says. "Job" may be the wrong word for what he does, but whatever you do, says Misha, "you should do it best."

And he does it best.

The impish, pale smooth face highlighted by soft blond hair and Baltic blue eyes conceals a computer-sharp mind. For it is behind those eyes with their dark, dramatic shadows, inside his head, that the control center of the superb athlete's body lies. The sharp intelligence that is the driver sits there.

In 1976, Baryshnikov did something "really new"—Twyla Tharp's *Push Comes to Shove*. The off-balance movement of the ballet was utterly foreign to his classically trained body.

And a masterful driver it must be to control the jumps, the stops, the 180-degree turns, the *cabrioles,* and *grands ballonnés,* the *grands jetés.* The extraordinary way he seems to hover in midair.

How does he do it?

"It's normal," he says, shrugging it off, disdainful of the long preparation involved, the extreme effort needed.

To Baryshnikov, the steps are just classical steps. Although they are difficult, he treats them almost as commonplace: "You see them all the time."

The height of his jumps, how many turns he does, or how fast he can do them — that is not the point.

The *grand jeté,* in fact, is not one of his favorite steps. And he complains that the public is insatiable. They want more and more.

Does he do ten pirouettes now? Perhaps next year he will do twelve.

He is afraid the public thinks of him as a machine.

Yet no one could accuse Misha of being a machine. The life he exudes could not come from such an objective entity. But his body is a finely honed, precisely tuned instrument. In that sense, he *is* a machine, a magnificent machine.

He came to the dance physically prepared, having flirted with gymnastics, but the long, grueling hours of energy-filled time he spent in classes really shaped and strengthened his body. It gave him the physical skills he needed, the skills he now displays with such seeming ease.

He is the greatest male classical dancer of his day.

He may be the greatest dancer ever.

In execution Baryshnikov combines a rare blend of two kinds of dancers.

The first displays the nuts and bolts and underpinnings of his craft.

The second makes it all *seem* effortless, concealing the workings under a solid chassis of smoothly flowing lines.

Baryshnikov certainly conceals the great power and speed needed to achieve those stunning virtuoso feats — the *grands ballonnés,* those astounding leaps high up toward the rafters; the *cabrioles,* when his legs beat gracefully together in midair; and the *grands jetés,* those leaps where he barely seems to touch the ground before bounding up again.

No one can do them like he can.

He even combines a seemingly impossible series of movements, as in the *grand jeté en tournant battan.* Leaping high into the air, he turns 180 degrees; then, while moving backward with his legs leading, beats them together twice in a scissorlike motion before lightly landing.

And he makes it look so easy.

He understates the supreme effort with which he pulls off the seemingly impossible while retaining the correct, classroom ideal in the line of his body.

It is not usual for a male dancer to keep his classic line. It is more often dropped while jumping or moving.

The loss of the correct body position is a part of the style of the first kind of dancer, the dancer who lets the audience see the machinery, the bare bones of the movement, the muscles straining to achieve the *grand ballonné,* or the double *tour en l'air,* in which the dancer revolves two full turns in a blur of motion.

Most dancers do it in a blur of motion. Only Baryshnikov appears to slow it down. The air around him jells, supporting his body. He is buoyant.

It is all an illusion, of course. Gravity tugs at him just as strongly as it does at any other dancer, and it takes an incredible amount of power to make the movement seem so easy, so graceful, so controlled.

Audiences sympathetically strain when they see the dancer strain, and they applaud the fact of gravity so visibly overcome.

There is an emotional tie between the ballet audience and the dancer, just as there often is in the sports arena. People in the audience rise from their seats as the athlete skims over the bar in the high jump. They tense their arms and backs as they struggle with the weightlifter to set a new record. They mirror the tension in Bruce Jenner's face as he puts forth his utmost to win the decathlon championship.

The physical empathy is greater when the audiences can see the effort vividly displayed, but the intellectual awe is lacking. The line is less classic, less perfect. The magic is diluted.

In Baryshnikov's case, although he telegraphs the supreme power involved, the ease with which he executes the movements makes it seem as if he is hardly trying.

He floats — as that other famed dancer, Muhammad Ali, might say — like a butterfly.

And he always, always keeps his body in perfect line.

He projects both the emotion and the intellectual awe.

It is this rare ability that makes Baryshnikov unique. And this uniqueness has helped him propel dance to the unprecedented popularity it is currently enjoying in America.

In 1965, four years after Rudolf Nureyev astonished the West with his explosive, heroic style, the total dance audience in this country was estimated at one million.

Respectable, but still rather exclusive when spread among the many American dance companies.

But by 1972, two years before Baryshnikov came upon the scene, something had happened. The most popular event on campus was not a rock concert, nor a sports event; it was a dance performance. The national audience for dance had grown to eleven million.

And in 1978, the figure had reached fifteen million and was climbing. Why?

The fame of key ballet figures such as Baryshnikov helped, but people were also discovering that the ballet held all the excitement and splendor of the sports arena. Seething, at times, with a civilized and peaceful ferment. Also, there was usually a story line. The most popular ballets have a story line. And ballet had the appeal of art. Of beauty.

The ballet is the utmost extension of one of our most primitive instincts — the need to dance. From the caveman pounding his feet in a ritualized celebration of the hunt, through the rain dance of the American Indian, the days of jitterbugs, twisters, and disco junkies, to the perfection of Baryshnikov.

That's it!

How much farther can dance go?

Of course, not everyone takes to the ballet. Then again, not everyone takes to baseball, or football, or the opera, or great literature.

In his novel *Kalki,* Gore Vidal has one of his characters utter the philosophy of one who does not subscribe to a season at the ABT.

"Next to mime," Vidal's character says, "I hate ballet. If there is a hell being prepared for me, it will be an eternity of watching Marcel Marceau alternate with the Bolshoi Ballet."

And neither the ballet, Nureyev, Balanchine, nor Baryshnikov has made it into the closely packed 1450-plus pages of *The People's Almanac.* Apparently father and son, Wallace and Wallechinsky, did not believe ballet to be a part of the culture of The People.

They're right. Ballet is still not a part of America's popular culture. It may be someday; it's come a long way from the turn of the century when, for all practical purposes, it didn't exist. But it still has a long way to go before it's truly popular.

In the early 1900s ballet was in a decline in the West. But in Russia it grew and prospered. In 1909, the Ballets Russes traveled from Saint Petersburg to Paris and stunned European audiences. Delighted them.

More! They wanted more.

The Ballets Russes gave them more and dominated the art of ballet for the next two decades.

Among the fantastic dancers in the Ballet Russe was one Vaslav Nijinsky, the greatest male dancer of his time.

There were other good male dancers around, but none was so brilliant

UPI Photo

as Nijinsky. None was brilliant enough to eclipse the ballerinas of the day. But Nijinsky could.

Of Nijinsky, the sculptor Rodin said, "His beauty is that of antique fresco and sculpture; he is the ideal model, whom one longs to draw and sculpt."

At the time Rodin saw him, Nijinsky was performing in his controversial ballet *The Afternoon of a Faun.* Controversial because the critics found the choreography too erotic.

"When the curtain rises to reveal him reclining on the ground," continued Rodin, "one knee raised, the pipe at his lips, you would think him a statue; and nothing could be more striking than the impulse with which, at the climax, he lies face down on the secreted veil, kissing it and hugging it to him with passionate abandon."

Meeting for the first time at a December 1974 party, Nureyev and Baryshnikov prepare to kiss in the Russian tradition. The party marked Nureyev's opening on Broadway with his own dance company.

The ABT production of *The Nutcracker* is Misha's own version of the Petipa ballet, in which he danced with ballerina Marianna Tcherkassky and later with Gelsey Kirkland. It is a ballet of special significance for Kirkland, who reexperienced childhood dancing it and enjoys it immensely.

It was this scene that brought forth prurient thoughts and opened forbidden doors in the critics' minds. They were scandalized by the twelve-minute ballet, just as the Russian Ministry of Culture was upset by the seminude Baryshnikov bounding about the stage in *The Creation of the World,* fifty years later.

Let us stop for a moment to analyze something. To give you a small idea of what a polished performance entails, *The Afternoon of a Faun* takes only twelve minutes to present, but it requires 120 rehearsals to perfect.

It is little wonder that Baryshnikov calls dancing very hard work.

The Russians, after Nijinsky, continued to produce outstanding dancers, many of them male. In the West — where there was ballet at all — the female dancers, the ballerinas, held the spotlight.

Partially this reflected the stigma that ballet carried for a male dancer. Was a good all-American boy going to grow up to be a ballet dancer?

Never.

He could be a baseball player or a doctor, a lawyer or an Indian chief — well, maybe not an Indian chief — or he could be out crushing bones on the football field. He could perform high jumps at a track meet.

As a result of this stigma, men who did become dancers suffered from two handicaps. First, they usually began their study late, after their bodies had developed and the flexibility they needed for the dance was gone. And, second, they had to overact, to be very *macho,* to compensate for the feminine stigma that being a dancer carried.

They danced in boldly masculine ways.

Edward Villella, for example, was an athletic dancer. He sacrificed purity of line for the expression of power. Villella looked and danced like an athlete. And an athlete was — at that time — considered absolutely masculine, above the suspicion of sexual ambivalence.

Not until the Russians came to our shores once more — Nureyev in '61 and Baryshnikov in '74 — did this feeling begin to change. Their superb technique and limber bodies seemed to prove that the dance could be a respectable art for a man.

Rudolf Nureyev brought a male animal magnetism, a sensual quality, to dance. He wasn't above showing off, either. He hammed it up, extended his princelike personality beyond the theater stage. He had a regal, sculptured quality. Disdainful.

Also, he was a good dancer.

He didn't, though, have the "one of the guys" image that Baryshnikov possessed.

Rudy was royalty.

Misha was people.

When Baryshnikov showed up in New York — hitherto Nureyev territory — he was twenty-six. Nureyev was ten years older.

Rudolf was approaching the years when his dancing would be less athletic and more stylistic. This usually comes to a male dancer at around the age of forty. By forty-five, male dancers are moving into character roles.

Would the young Baryshnikov take the spotlight away from Nureyev? Could they be friends? Or would the competition between the two men, and their respective personalities and talents, stand in their way?

There is "no competition between us whatsoever," Baryshnikov said in 1974.

Misha called Nureyev "a very great dancer." He termed it an honor to be dancing in New York while Nureyev was also performing in the city.

Nureyev said flattering things about Baryshnikov. Then.

Nureyev also denied trying to dance better than anyone else, trying to turn their dancing into a competition. He competed only against himself.

Nureyev called Baryshnikov "an extremely talented dancer." And he wished him well, adding that he hoped Baryshnikov would absorb the great ballet riches of the West.

The two men became friends, and Baryshnikov stayed in Nureyev's home when he traveled to London.

But the friendship cooled. A little over a year later, in November 1975, Nureyev's evaluation of his fellow expatriate reflected this change.

Admitting that their relationship was not as close as it had been earlier, Nureyev reminded people that there were other dancers around — he named Fernando Bujones and Anthony Dowell. Baryshnikov, he said, was not the only great dancer.

Perhaps Baryshnikov was stealing too much of Nureyev's thunder. Or it may have been simply the difference in life styles and attitudes.

Offstage — as well as on — Nureyev was, or could be, outrageous. Flamboyant.

Baryshnikov was not.

Rudy was a jet-setter, a trend-setter, a confidant of the social set. He seemed to glow in the flash of the cameras.

Misha was quieter. Seemingly more serious. ("I am very serious. I am serious man, really.")

He was partial to faded jeans and patterned shirts. He gave interviews, but reluctantly.

He was happier when he was left alone.

The cooling friendship between Misha and Rudy may have been caused by the constant comparison to which the two Russian dancers from the Kirov had been subjected.

Liza Minnelli and Mikhail perform their own version of *Saturday Night Fever* at New York's celebrated Studio 54 in January 1978.

Things that Nureyev and Baryshnikov had in common were often cited. They were both perfectionists. They both took risks on stage. Yet, as Laurence Olivier once observed, nothing is really interesting in the theater unless the actor "risks sudden death."

To Baryshnikov, that was not quite true. He did not feel that the actor or dancer must think he is risking sudden death. Only the audience should feel that he is.

In any case, comparisons between Rudy and Misha pointed out their differences more than their similarities. For instance, in the ballet *Giselle,* Nureyev played the lead male role as it is usually interpreted. Albrecht, the count, was a cad.

Albrecht is aristocratic and authoritarian. In explaining how the role is usually interpreted, Baryshnikov called his social position and noble bearing the "most important aspects" of the role.

That is not the way he danced it.

He did not see Albrecht that way. Baryshnikov envisioned an Albrecht who was sincere. Who was a little naive, boyish. How else could the boyish Baryshnikov play it? And his Albrecht was innocently, thoroughly, in love.

In *Giselle,* the romantic ballet that premiered in Paris in 1841, Count Albrecht disguises himself as a peasant in order to win the favors of a beautiful peasant girl, Giselle. She falls in love with the Count, who keeps his nobility a secret from her.

Albrecht has a rival for Giselle's heart — Hilarion. Discovering who Albrecht really is, Hilarion jealously tries to break up the romance of the star-crossed lovers by revealing Albrecht's identity. And also revealing the fact that Albrecht is betrothed to another, a girl of his own class.

When Giselle learns the truth, she goes mad and dies. And because she has died before her wedding day, she has to join the Wilis, the restless spirits of unmarried maidens. But she saves her lover, Albrecht, from his romantic fate, to dance on for all eternity.

Giselle has been called "an old warhorse of a romantic ballet" and "a tearjerker." Whatever one might think of it, the ballet has become one of the most successful of all time.

Giselle was important to Baryshnikov because many people did not believe he could dance it. He was too young for the role. His short and slightly chunky body did not fit the streamlined image most people had of Albrecht.

He was nervous and tense during rehearsals for the ballet. He practiced daily with Natalia Makarova, who was his partner in the dance.

Unlike many other ballet stars, who conserve energy by walking through their steps in a rehearsal, Baryshnikov usually dances every step.

Many times, this is unintentional, he says, "but the dancing takes over."

He pulled it off. In New York, on July 27, 1974, he made the boyish Albrecht live.

He was outstanding. His technique was effortless, his acting superb. His performance was poetic.

One orchestra member was so overcome that she nearly threw her violin onstage. Like all the other members of the audience that night, she was entranced by a dancer who had set out to do his best — and had done so.

What is the essence of all art? It is "to have pleasure in giving pleasure," says Baryshnikov.

Pleasure he has given. And pleasure he has received in return.

But, at times, he hates the dance.

When?

"After a bad performance." But this happens very rarely and his hatred of his work never lasts long.

Baryshnikov insists that he dances because he is happy. To him, the dance is "a light, giddy chill in my guts."

He still thrills to the applause as he did that first time in the Latvian school, but no matter how much applause and how many bravos he receives, there are always doubts that gnaw at his mind. Could he have done better? Was the heart-stopping brisé — the spectacular leg beats in the air that he has done so well — a personal affectation, or did it belong in the ballet?

He worries about the impression he has made after a performance. For the interpretation is his, even though the step is in the ballet. He calls it the "last gasp of the soul."

Whatever.

Who, other than a ballet master, could argue the point?

The first ballet created for him in the West was choreographed by John Butler to Samuel Barber's music. Medea was a dance full of frenzy, a dance of vengeance, a duet with Carla Fracci first performed in 1975 at Italy's Festival of Two Worlds in Spoleto.

The ballet combines both classic and modern steps, and it was the first ballet in which Baryshnikov performed not wearing tights. He found it fascinating and exciting. He had danced into the modern era, into the twenty-first century.

Finally.

He is very excited about roles that are created for him. He feels that they open up new and unrealized worlds.

Naturally, he has gained from dancing the classical repertory. But he longs to dance in ballets by Robbins, Balanchine, Tudor, MacMillan, and Petit. He wants to work with choreographers who believe he can dance in their ballets. He is willing to grant the choreographer the right over everything when the ballet is being created.

It was Baryshnikov in the classics that the audiences loved, but they would learn to appreciate his work in modern ballets, too. For, as Clive Barnes pointed out, he was born to dance everything.

"He dances like the wind of heaven."

He did dance in practically everything. Running through Tudor, Butler, Petit, Tharp, Tetley, Balanchine, and others. Sixteen new works were created for him. He mastered thirty new roles of varying scope. In just two years. He even worked freelance, in such numbers as *Pas de Duke* with Judith Jamison at Alvin Ailey's American Dance Theater. His freelance fees as an international star have brought him $10,000 for each performance.

He excelled in Twyla Tharp's *Push Comes to Shove,* a funny potpourri of jazz, disco, and classical ballet. He felt that the point of performing in such modern works was to see more. It would open doors for him, would aid him in adding new depths to his already fathomless style.

He was especially interested in doing ballets that incorporated the Martha Graham mode of dancing. He didn't know that school of dancing. And Alvin Ailey used it.

He worried about "all the contractions in the stomach" that Ailey wanted. He felt he couldn't do them well. Yet he was willing to try because it was an interesting situation for him.

He found it difficult to combine his classical training with the quick jazz steps and confessed that at first he felt like "a cow."

Antony Tudor also presented a challenge for him. Here the challenge was mental, not technical. He had to know exactly what he was dancing about. Not simply think it on stage. Know it.

Baryshnikov never forgets that the dancer is performing for an audience. He knows how important it is not to forget that.

He realizes his dancing is not disco dancing. He is not dancing only for himself. He must dance to the ballet and to the audience.

In Russia, the connection with the theater and the audience was strong. He could understand their reaction. He knew how they would like certain things, what other dancers would say. He also hoped they would like what he did.

Or at least, he hoped, they would not hate it.

Even with a great artist, there are sometimes uncertainties. There is a need for approval.

As an artist, Baryshnikov prefers ballets with a good dramatic plan. Be-

cause of this, he likes ballets with a good story.

Even so, he is not enamored of *Swan Lake*, one of the most famous ballets. Nevertheless, he did like Erik Bruhn's production of the ballet. Siegfried had more scenes than in any other version and Bruhn made the prince a much more active participant in the drama.

Baryshnikov danced in Bruhn's production in Canada in September 1975, with Nadia Potts.

Bruhn remembers when Baryshnikov came to the National Ballet of Canada in 1975. It was there that he danced his first *Swan Lake*. Bruhn taught him the role of the Prince in his production of the ballet. All the while he coached him in the role, he found it hard to believe that he had actually danced the role himself. "Did I really do that?" he kept thinking. He had completely disassociated himself from a character he had por-

The classicist Baryshnikov was especially interested in learning the Martha Graham mode of dancing. Alvin Ailey used it for *Pas de Duke*, for which Misha danced free-lance with Judith Jamison.

When dancing in Ailey's flashy, fun *Pas de Duke*, Baryshnikov
worried about "all those contractions in the stomach." He
couldn't do them well. He lacked the smooth fluidity that
Jamison brought to the dance, he felt, and confessed that he
sometimes looked like a cow. But the jazzy, blues
construction captured his imagination and his performance
was beautiful and poetic.

trayed often. He calls it an "odd sensation" but also a "relief."

Baryshnikov says that he would probably never have danced in *Swan Lake* had he stayed in the Soviet Union. He didn't care for the Kirov presentation of the ballet. He thought it too massive and grand. He also felt that the role of Siegfried had a tendency to get lost. Baryshnikov prefers a role that is central to the ballet; he doesn't care for one that is "just a prop."

It's not that he disagrees with choreographers who stress the role of the male dancer as a lifter of the ballerinas.

To a point, he believes in this approach. But he also believes that the role of the male dancer — in order to be a good role — must be essential to the plot.

He has been lucky in his selection of dance partners. Gelsey Kirkland and Natalia Makarova are splendid examples. Baryshnikov calls them "great individuals." His relationships with each ballerina have been different — the mental contact, the physical situation. It has been "very exciting for me," Baryshnikov says in tribute to the ballerinas.

"And I hope," he adds, "for them, too."

Undoubtedly.

Once, joking, he said that the only qualification he looked for in a partner was that she didn't step on his toes. Then, relenting somewhat in this severe restriction, he said he might even overlook that if, when she did, she said, "Sorry." An urchin grin lit up his face.

His partners are good even when they dance with others, but ABT director Lucia Chase says, "Everybody dances better when he's around."

When Misha first came to America, he had no plans to do his own productions, especially not to choreograph them. It was difficult enough to dance and do ballet. Also, he felt that great dancers do not always make great choreographers. The reverse was also true, he said.

But he found that it was not all that difficult after all. Although he still did not consider himself a choreographer, merely a restager or producer. He worked on a Baryshnikov version of *The Nutcracker,* which was presented nationally over CBS-TV, and a shortened, Broadway-type version of a Russian favorite, *Don Quixote.*

He called *Don Q.* "a mess," but added, "I love it."

Baryshnikov was not the first to fiddle with the choreography of the Petipa ballet. The version he tackled was an oft-tampered-with one. Through the years, dancers and choreographers have added or taken away something from the original until it has become more of less a showcase of dancers' specialties.

Although based on the Cervantes tale of the errant knight and his faithful companion, they are incidental characters to the plot. The story, essentially, is that of the lusty barber Basilio, and his pursuit of Kitri, the innkeeper's daughter.

Don Q. is noted for its uproarious comedy, its drama, and its many folk sequences. And it contains some excellent virtuoso passages for the principal dancers.

If the ballet is as much of a mess as Baryshnikov claims, why did he bother with this "crazy Russian salad of a ballet?"

Anticipating the question, he asked reporters if they had wondered why he had bothered to stage it.

It was not a great ballet, yet Russians adore it.

Well produced, Baryshnikov added, the ballet had "style, charm, and a genuine atmosphere." He liked it, too, because it demanded more than academic technique, and it assuredly demanded that. A successful *Don Quixote*, according to Baryshnikov, demanded "stage presence, mimetic ability, and comic flair."

He starred in his own production and succeeded admirably, since he possessed all the necessary qualifications for success, especially the "comic flair." He has a natural ability to play the clown, which he has displayed in unaffected delight in other ballets, including *Push Comes to Shove.*

Maybe this is not great ballet, but it is fun, and in the way Misha re-staged it as "classic vaudeville," the fun is enhanced.

He cut it and edited it in such a way that it was as well paced as a Broadway show. He shaped it to conform to what he believed was "American taste."

Whether or not he succeeded in his intention is a matter for the critics and audiences to decide — or for posterity. But it was a lively, enjoyable, fast-paced version.

But he had had enough of producing for a while. After *Don Quixote,* he planned no more Baryshnikov productions. He wanted to dance for a while, in different ballets. In a different company.

Dancing is a necessity for him. When he is not working, he feels "off balance." He works hard, in the realization that life is short. He will relax later. When? "When I stop dancing."

When he was dancing at the Kirov, he spent most of his time dancing nineteenth-century ballets. After he came to America and the ABT, he still spent a lot of time in those ballets. Finally, it was enough.

In April 1978, he announced that he would henceforth be dancing with Balanchine's City Ballet.

He had wanted to work with the master choreographer, Balanchine, from the beginning.

Now he had made his move.

Photograph © Lois Greenfield

Push Comes to Shove is a serious dance, says the number-one fan of choreographer Tharp. In it she so integrates the music with the movements that everything is logical and beautiful. Tharp, Misha says, is a "genius," and he felt he had never worked so hard to learn a dance. It was to him as if he went "to the moon and back again." With Misha in *Push Comes to Shove* are Clark Tippet, left, and Marianna Tcherkassky.

Back Home
En Arrière

I want to dance in Balanchine ballets."
Baryshnikov spoke those words not long after he made his great leap to the West in 1974. But instead of landing at the City Ballet with Balanchine, he placed his feet firmly on the stage of the American Ballet Theatre and made a four-year stopover.

Nevertheless, those words kept echoing through rehearsal halls; he could not shake the intensity of the thought; the idea continued to haunt him, daring him.

Finally he had to do it. He had to join Balanchine's company.

He had dreamed of joining for a long time. But he held back. He wasn't sure of Balanchine's reaction. He did not want to be a dancer the choreographer didn't want to have.

The desire may have always been there, and Baryshnikov may have stated many, many times that he wanted more than anything in the world to dance in Balanchine ballets. Nevertheless, the move astonished the dance world.

Rocked it, some said.

Should those fans who want to see him dance in the classics buy tickets to the New York City Ballet? No. "Go see *The Turning Point*," he says.

72

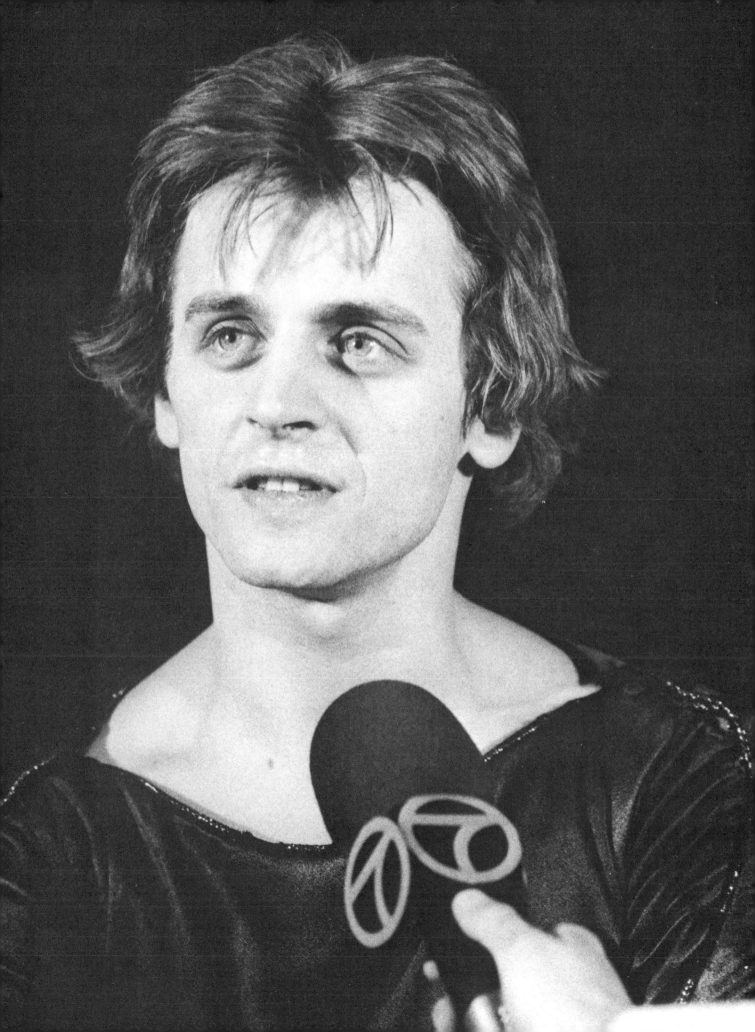

Why had Baryshnikov done it? Why had he traded fame and fortune for the fragile honor of dancing for the master?

It definitely wasn't for money. His earnings at City Ballet would be far less than the $3,500 a performance he was getting at the ABT. Salaries at City Ballet run more like $750 a *week*.

That's quite a pay cut.

Then, maybe he doesn't need money now. Maybe he has enough money. After all, when you earn more than $200,000 a year, maybe you just aren't all that interested in making more money.

Baryshnikov, echoing the past, called it an artistic decision. It was the same sentiment he had used in explaining his defection from the Soviet Union four years earlier.

The decision was a long time brewing, but it went from simmer to boil as he became bored with what he was doing, and more and more appreciative of Balanchine's work.

Misha called Balanchine's ballets "very wonderful" no matter how they were danced. "I need his choreography more than it needs me," Misha said in 1976, two years before he made his momentous decision.

After the April announcement he indicated the depth of his boredom with non-Balanchine ballets. He related how tired he was of ballets in which he was merely on display, ones in which critics had nothing more to write about than the shape he was in.

He had begun to have little talks with himself. "To be, or not to be," as in *Hamlet.*

"I decided to be," says Baryshnikov.

The decision was all Misha's. Balanchine did not beg him to join.

Balanchine denied casting any lures at Baryshnikov. He said that Misha just wanted to dance with their company. Like everyone else. At one time Nureyev had expressed a wish to dance with City Ballet, to do *Giselle* and *Swan Lake.* Balanchine had said, "When you get tired of them, then you come here."

But Nureyev never got tired.

Balanchine felt that it was too expensive for Nureyev and Baryshnikov to go to City Ballet. They don't pay anything compared to other companies. Balanchine had come from the same place as Rudy and Misha and he had never made any money. Even when he worked on Broadway. He could see that the two great dancers must first make some money, dancing everywhere. If they did not, they would starve in the ballet world.

Was that what Baryshnikov had set out to do? Make his bundle and then be an "artist"?

Who could blame him if that were true?

But it wasn't.

The reason he did not join Balanchine immediately, he said, was because he was "emotionally upset and bewildered."

He did not know what to do.

It was Natalia Makarova — a woman he had known for ten years — who invited him to join the ABT. And he was grateful for the marvelous opportunity. But as soon as he performed for the ABT, he felt it was too late to join the City Ballet. Because Mr. Balanchine wouldn't be first.

Baryshnikov also needed to look around. He wanted to scout out the territory and see just what was happening. He had to make sure that he understood Balanchine's point of view about dancing.

He had once asked Balanchine about dancing his ballets in Europe. Balanchine reminded him, not without irony, that his public expected him to do the "glamorous thing."

Baryshnikov felt that Balanchine was telling him to do his thing and let Balanchine do his.

The public does expect Baryshnikov to do his "glamorous thing." Many fans will be disappointed with the Baryshnikov who will be performing at top speed, executing the sharp, quick footwork in the abstract City Ballet productions.

Balanchine's choreography is difficult. That fact alone should present enough excitement to appease the high-priced ticketholders. But it probably won't. Not all of them, anyway.

Does Baryshnikov really care if they are appeased?

No.

He wants to dance in Balanchine's ballets. When he does, the audience will know what they are going to see. To that part of the public that is disappointed at not seeing him in *Don Quixote* or *Giselle,* Baryshnikov says, "Don't come."

Perhaps they can see him in *The Turning Point.*

At the American Ballet Theatre, the dancers are more important than the ballets. At the New York City Ballet, it is the opposite. Popular recognition and money are offered to ABT stars. The City Ballet offers far less in concrete terms, but for Baryshnikov, it is far more. It is the chance to work with the master.

The master and his new student share a common ballet legacy. George Balanchine, a native of Saint Petersburg, graduated from the Imperial Maryinsky Ballet School and joined the Maryinsky Ballet. That was in 1921, before the Maryinsky's name was changed to Kirov and Saint Petersburg became Leningrad.

Both men started from the same gate.

"We went through the same school," Balanchine acknowledges. "He

Christine Sarry and Baryshnikov in rehearsal (above) and in a performance of Feld's *Variations on America*, a seven-minute romp, full of vitality and good humor.

Photograph © Lois Greenfield

The score for *Variations on America*, originally a Charles Ives organ fantasia, was orchestrated by William Schuman. It is, Feld said, "a series of opinions" full of optimism. Performed in March 1977 by Sarry and Baryshnikov, the ballet demands speed and lucidity because of its incredible compression. It is, after all, two hundred years of history presented in seven minutes—an apple-pie, blue-eyed, sunny look at America.

Photograph © Lois Greenfield

likes to point his feet and do beats. It's all very classical.''

When he made the change in ballet companies, Baryshnikov became the first dancer from the Soviet Union to join Balanchine's company. He feels that this move is a homecoming of sorts. It will be like going back to the Kirov. Back to the 200-year-old Russian tradition of ballet.

In Russia ballet education is a very serious business. The focus is on classical ballet, mime, and character dancing. Dancers in the West come from many kinds of schools — private classes, New York City ballet schools, and schools in remote parts of the country. Each teacher has a different background and point of view. Many different versions of classical ballet are taught — Danish, Italian, French, and new American. The Russians have but one discipline, and education in the dance in Russia is not informal.

"I am going back," Baryshnikov says of his move to Balanchine, "and still going forward."

Going back because Balanchine's base is one of strict classicism. Going forward because Balanchine has refined and polished his ballets to such a degree that they have been transformed from classical to modern. They stress speed, agility, and a startling angularity. The music evokes the dance. Movement is everything. The story, if any, is incidental. But the underlying form is pure.

It is, Misha says, classical dance in the great Russian tradition of Petipa. But Balanchine has developed a new kind of ballet theater, one that never existed before.

But, Baryshnikov adds, the flow of the choreography at the City Ballet is such that there is no preparation for movements. In the standard nineteenth-century ballets, there is time to prepare.

Gelsey Kirkland has commented on this difference. She should know. She did what Baryshnikov has done, only in reverse. First to Balanchine, then to the ABT. If you watch Baryshnikov before he jumps, she says, then slow down a film of the jump, you will see that it's almost like a pole vaulter's jump. The natural power of the torso is being used.

He won't be doing that anymore.

Although Misha enjoyed working with modern choreographers such as Alvin Ailey and Twyla Tharp, he felt for the past year or so that the work was becoming repetitious. It was tiring to go through the same routines he has been through for twelve years.

It will certainly be a change for him. The New York City Ballet is a special world with special laws and a special philosophy.

Baryshnikov declares it "a privilege" to work with Balanchine. He calls himself, and happily so, an "instrument" in Balanchine's hands.

It was in April of 1978 that Balanchine and Baryshnikov sat down together to seriously discuss the change. They met in Balanchine's apartment.

Baryshnikov had signaled the meeting, had made overtures. Balanchine responded with the invitation to his apartment and it was settled.

The settlement amounted to this: There would be no special allowances made for the star. If he wanted to join, he had to join permanently. "We don't have guest artists," Balanchine said.

After one year, Baryshnikov would be free to leave. Dancers who sign contracts with Balanchine sign for a year at a time. They are not made to feel they are in prison. Free to go, they usually stay.

"I'm glad that he's coming," Balanchine confesses. He is very pleased. Not because he is getting a superstar, but because he is getting a dancer.

Although Baryshnikov can appear as a guest star elsewhere, just as any other dancer from Balanchine's company can, he will not be dancing with other ballet companies in New York City.

And there is an acknowledged "no-star" policy at the NYCB. But that hardly perturbs superstar Baryshnikov.

"I never called myself a star," he says. "I'm a dancer."

He realizes it won't be easy for him, but he feels that he can find himself in Balanchine's choreography. He hopes to find a new attitude toward the public, a new aspect of his entire professional life.

He does not want to talk about what he is giving up. He would rather discuss what he is getting.

Was it true, as rumors suggested, that Balanchine was looking for a successor? Balanchine is seventy-four, and although immortal in one sense, he is certainly mortal in another. Is he planning to groom Baryshnikov to be his successor? It seems unlikely.

But Baryshnikov will be getting the benefit of years of experience from one of the founders of twentieth-century dance. Perhaps only Martha Graham has exerted as much influence on modern dance as has Balanchine.

The City Ballet also has some excellent dancers — Edward Villella, Peter Martins, Patricia McBride, and the upcoming Heather Watts, to name a few — and a wonderful repertory of ballets.

No one knows what form ballet will take a quarter of a century from now. *Giselle* and *Swan Lake* will probably still be around, but for the rest it is hard to say.

Balanchine, along with Jerome Robbins, has inspired a whole generation of choreographers. Their influence will undoubtedly be felt. Which of them will be the most influential? No one can know for sure. Not too many new young choreographers are around. Beyond Balanchine's and Robbins's works, which will survive, the future is uncertain.

Jerome Robbins, who also made the shift from the ABT to the City Ballet, was not surprised to hear of Baryshnikov's decision to join them.

He called City Ballet a "serious company" and saw it as a place for "serious artists."

Neither was Natalia Makarova shocked. She cited the artistic growth all great dancers seek. She could understand and respect that desire. She felt that the ABT had become routine for Baryshnikov.

But Makarova felt that nobody could replace him at the ABT. "Misha is Misha," she said.

She did not know if she could have done the same thing. She is not ready to separate herself from the classics. She needs them, she said, emotionally. And the "exclusive" policy that the NYCB demands seems strange to her.

Russian artists who made leaps to the West thought they would have total artistic freedom. But they reckoned without ballet politics. For example, they learned they could not dance with both the ABT and the New York City Ballet. They wonder why. They cannot understand why Balanchine does not ask them to join his company even for one season. They do not see how this could hurt anything.

But, all that aside, Makarova is happy for Misha. She feels he knows what he is doing. And dancing the wonderful Balanchine and Robbins ballets will "certainly enrich his art."

Whatever happens to Baryshnikov, his presence at the NYCB will not affect the company.

"Why should it?" Balanchine asks. Baryshnikov will merely be an additional member, one very good new dancer for the company. When so many get sick, "it's good to have someone healthy."

How quickly will Misha fit into the company?

Balanchine will decide what ballets will be good for Misha. And what ballets Misha will do well in.

Baryshnikov danced gloriously in the company's Saratoga, New York, summer season in July 1978, after being with Balanchine for only a few weeks.

What the future will bring for both Misha and the City Ballet is an intriguing question. Will City Ballet, for instance, have to put up signs saying "Misha tickets all sold out," as the ABT did? Can a "no-star" policy really hide the glow of Baryshnikov's superstardom?

And would Gelsey Kirkland, who left Balanchine to dance with Baryshnikov, return to the fold?

The answer to that last question, at least, was supplied by "Mr. B."

"She is not coming," he said. "She can stay where she is."

Did he actually say that? Or was he misquoted? Gelsey does not feel

Photograph © Lois Greenfield

that sounded like Balanchine. She wonders exactly what he said. She cannot believe he would hold what she did against her.

In any case, Gelsey is contented where she is. "I know this is where I want to be."

That doesn't mean, though, that she has lost any respect for either Balanchine or his ballets. She admits that when she sees a "glorious Balanchine ballet," she wants to get up and dance it. But the new ballets she has danced have become a part of her. She is happy.

Baryshnikov wants the ballets to become a part of him, too.

He is now thirty. At thirty-five, he feels the change would come too late. Even at thirty-two.

He knows he is still young and "quick to learn new things."

And, as Gelsey Kirkland once remarked, "Working with first-class people makes you more first-class yourself."

Old friend Natalia Makarova is happy for Misha. Dancing the Balanchine ballets will "enrich his art." But nobody can replace him at the ABT. "Misha is Misha."

Frank Sinatra sings (on record) for Twyla Tharp's *Once More, Frank*. Here she dances her own choreography with Misha. Twyla created the ballet for the two of them for a special ABT gala performance. It was a unique experience for Misha to be in a ballet in which the choreographer also danced.

Photograph © Lois Greenfield

Time,
Pain, and Stress
Coda

He's thirty now.

At twenty-nine he gave himself only six or seven more years of dancing on the stage.

After that he did not know what he would do. He knew that his body was stiffer, stronger, and not as flexible as a ballerina's body. Also, he had jumped and expended much more energy than a ballerina.

When a male dancer reaches the age of thirty-five, his muscles no longer respond as readily. That's when the real pressure begins.

Thirty, in professional dance terms, is like fifty in ordinary terms. It's also true for athletes, especially those who are in sports that demand great physical stamina and strain. But, for dancers, the stress increases not only from wear and tear and age, but also from choreographers who are busy devising new ballets that are more demanding physically.

Baryshnikov does not plan to kill himself. "When it will be natural, I stop without regret," he once said.

He paraphrases a popular cigarette commercial of a few years back:

The tremendous physical stress on a dancer's body is similar to that on an athlete's. All the hazards that plague the sports star haunt the ballet idol.

"It's not how long you make it, it's how you make it . . . and what."

Again like an athlete, a dancer can burn himself out before his time if he doesn't take care of his body. He has to be constantly in training; a short layoff can hurt the performance. The dancer must keep in top shape at all times.

Dancers are, without a doubt, the "best-conditioned athletes," dancer Ted Kivitt states. If they skip practice for a week, they are totally out of shape.

Ted was thirty-two when Misha entered the ranks of the ABT. It was likely that Baryshnikov took some of the glow from Kivitt's career at the time. Ted thinks so.

But it didn't keep him from dancing, and dancing well. It simply took away some of the spotlight, some of the recognition. Ted is now in the prime of his dancing. Actually, he's at the end of his prime. Being realistic at thirty-six, he is appraising the future.

He admits that age is hard on male dancers. But there are parts for older men, parts that have a certain maturity about them. And dancing character roles often requires more technique.

Nevertheless, he claims the best insurance against too early an old age is to take good care of yourself.

There is, of course, no real insurance against the ravages of age.

And so age, sprains, twisted backs — all the hazards that plague an athlete — haunt the dancer. Even dancers with as much stamina as Baryshnikov.

In his first year in the West there was much pressure, which may have accounted for a lot of injuries. Since then he has learned a lot and his body protects itself mechanically. As he says, "I'm trying to survive."

A great many more performances are demanded of a star principal in the United States than in Russia. There, a dancer would perform maybe five times a month. Here, it could be as many as five times a week.

Besides performing, dancers like Baryshnikov take a daily ninety-minute ballet class. And if he is preparing for a new ballet, he will have to rehearse as much as six or seven hours a day. The schedule is altered on the day of the performance. An hour of rest is planned before the curtain goes up.

Even if he is completely exhausted after a performance, twelve hours later he must rehearse for a new role. His body has little chance to recuperate. At times he feels terrible, even with massages.

If he dances two ballets in one evening, he must have ten hours' sleep. A half day later he must be ready for his next rehearsal. Sometimes he performs on the same day he rehearses for another ballet the day after. You can "go bananas," Baryshnikov says.

Misha usually gets one free day a month. He spends it either sleeping or fishing.

Anything to ease the pressure on his body.

In January 1975, while on a tour of Australia, he seriously strained a tendon in his ankle. He was able to finish the *pas de deux* from *Don Quixote*, which he was dancing with Natalia Makarova. But after two curtain calls, he passed out.

The ankle caused him pain long after he was allowed out of bed and had cast off his crutches.

At the time of the injury, he admitted he was "running on nervous energy." He said he was working on relieving that situation.

But he was just entering his new life, he was not there yet. With no set schedule and no organization, only nervous energy sustained him.

President Carter joined Washington's elite at the premiere of Baryshnikov's *Don Quixote*. Misha was "superb," said Carter, but Gelsey Kirkland got the kiss.

Time, Pain, and Stress—Coda   89

Later that year, he had begun to adapt, and was "asking for more and more performances."

As Baryshnikov has discovered often, the stress that a dancer can impose on his body is tremendous. And it can lead to injury.

Greg Osborne, twenty-three, an aspiring soloist at the ABT, knows both the bad and the good sides of dance training. He began studying ballet when he was ten. It wasn't because he was hooked on the dance; he did it for therapy. When he was nine he broke both his legs in a childhood accident. He had to wear the casts for six months, and the leg muscles had weakened. The following fall he went into ballet. Dance can be excellent physical therapy.

Since then, except for the usual sprains and strains, the only major injury he has experienced was a knee injury that resulted from a heavy schedule. He had been running from class to rehearsal to performance, "trying to do everything at once." He didn't warm up properly one evening and still tried to do the performance full-out. He hurt his knee.

He was out for two weeks, and it took six weeks before he could feel at ease when dancing. He danced most of the six weeks, but "very, very carefully."

How soon an injured dancer can dance again depends on the injury. Many dancers resume quickly without hurting themselves.

But there is pain. Dancers deal with pain all the time.

Edward Villella says that male dancers are under as much pressure as any athlete. The strength required to get through a six-minute *pas de deux* is greater than that needed for four rounds of boxing.

When Baryshnikov arrived in Washington, D.C., in April 1978 for the first performance of his *Don Quixote,* he was drained. His energy had been sapped by a hard seventeen-week tour. Besides directing and starring in the ballet, he had to attend company production meetings that lasted until three in the morning. Schedules were off; everyone was running, working at a frenetic pace. Still, the first full run-through of the ballet took place only two days before the premiere.

American ballet is demanding.

But to relax is difficult. Misha realizes that. He knows it is important to schedule things sensibly and not to overdo. But he likens himself to a horse that is used to pulling a great load. He can't begin to imagine what would happen if he stopped dancing.

He tries hard not to think about a future without the dance. He called the stage "a form of opium" for him. He must have it. He cannot do without it.

It was during that hectic Washington season that the Kitri of the evening, ballerina Martine van Hamel, fell on stage and injured her leg. It was

Santa Fe Saga, **with its Mexican-flavored score, gave Baryshnikov a multiplicity of character roles to perform in the high-stepping ballet.**

Photograph © Lois Greenfield

twenty minutes into the performance.

Fortunately, Baryshnikov was in the audience. He located his partner, Gelsey Kirkland, at a restaurant, and called her back to the theater. Together, she and Baryshnikov finished the performance.

Gelsey has also had her share of physical troubles. One time was at the Balanchine company, when she was given the chance to dance *Theme and Variations*. Balanchine had revised it and made it even more intricate than it had been.

Although she danced beautifully, the pressure of doing the steps caused her to develop tendonitis.

She loves dancing more than anything in the world, but she could not dance with the pain.

Dancing ballet is unnatural for the body. Toes are bruised, ankles are

Photograph © Lois Greenfield

twisted, small bones are cracked. But, as Gelsey points out, as unnatural as dancing is, "you have to find a natural way of doing the unnatural."

Some dancers manage to do this better than others. The ones who do are given the credit they deserve.

Americans are a people in motion and they admire fitness, as Charles Fischl, general manager of the Atlanta Ballet, once remarked. People who recognize ballet as grueling admire its athletic side.

Maybe it's because of this intense, unrelenting pressure that many ballet dancers live in such a closed-off world; a world that could magnify psychological stresses. Again, something that the ballet dancer shares with the athlete.

Mark Spitz trained for twelve years to become an Olympic champion. And although he realized his ambition, he lost something in the pro-

Set in a frontier town of the Old West, *Santa Fe Saga* transformed the classical ballet star into a swaggering, macho cowboy, an Indian scout, an aristocratic badman, and a Mexican peasant. It was not the best ballet he had ever danced, but it was one of the liveliest.

cess — a social ease away from the pool and the competition. He was less well equipped than he might have been to meet the majority of the world that lives on dry land.

Dancers have a similar problem.

Many of them live as if they were locked inside a box. That is their world and they know nothing outside it. "I try not to be like that," says Edward Villella.

The day never ends for a dancer.

If he goes to a dinner party, he restricts himself to one drink, maybe two. He can't drink too much because his next role is always a demanding one. And before he can dance it, he must plan the many things directly associated with the dancing. Nevertheless, he is a happy man, both in his professional and personal life. He feels "very privileged" to be able to do what he likes to do.

Even Baryshnikov, for all his periods of gloom and his tendency to moan, "It's impossible," goes on. And does the impossible.

He recognizes that there is a time in a young artist's life when he must bring something of himself to the stage, something deep from within. And it must be there to begin with if he is to bring it out. Performers who are well trained but not morally disciplined fall apart.

Baryshnikov has also been heard to mutter about "the moral preparation" he has to endure in the perfection of a new role.

He says he is not yet a dancer. He is in the process of becoming. He is still learning.

He admits he has made many mistakes. But they are his mistakes. He has planned his life, sometimes refusing to do things, and being right about his refusal. And sometimes refusing to do things, and being wrong.

He feels he must manage his life. It would be "terrible" at the end to say, "My God! This fellow who was responsible for my life. He was wrong."

He trusts his own taste more than that of others. He conducts his own life. When he is wrong he is free to say, "Is your mistake, you stupid dummy." He is talking to himself.

It takes a special kind of person to be a dancer. They have to give up much. But a talented, dedicated dancer such as Mikhail Baryshnikov gains a lot also. Fame, fortune, respect, the sense of fulfillment that comes from achieving what you dreamed of, and the indescribable joy of being able to earn your living by doing what you love to do most of all.

Misha has that.

What else could anyone ask?

"Health." He is serious. Just for a moment.

"And also," he grins, "a good lunch."

The 1978 *Dance Magazine* award was presented to a clowning Baryshnikov by a delighted Judith Jamison. The award, given to Jamison in 1972, honors the top creative talent in the field of dance.

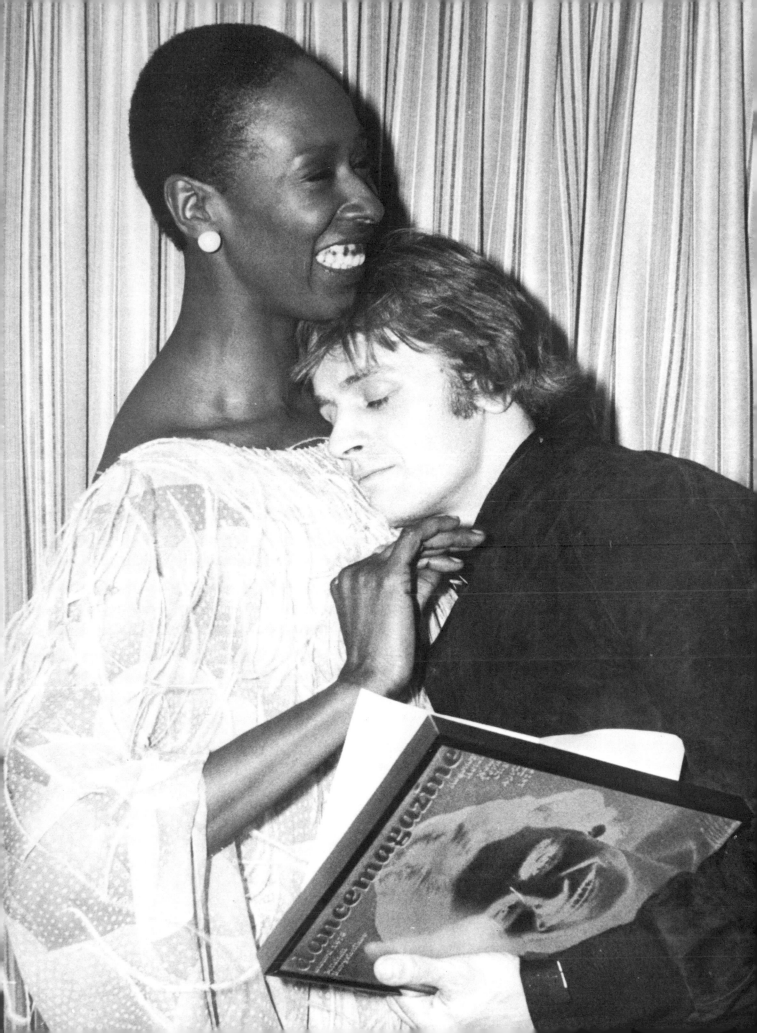

Index